# One Pair
# of Boots

# One Pair of Boots
## Land's End to John O'Groats

*by*

Tony Hobbs

with illustrations *by* Gill Simonds
& photographs *by* Tony Hobbs

**Tony Hobbs**
*in association with*
**Logaston Press**

LOGASTON PRESS
Little Logaston, Logaston, Woonton,
Almeley, Herefordshire HR3 6QH


First published by Logaston Press 2000
Copyright © Tony Hobbs 2000

ISBN 1 873827 41 5


Set in Times by Logaston Press
and printed in Great Britain by
The Cromwell Press, Trowbridge

*Cover illustrations:*
*Front: Hadrian's Wall looking towards Milecastle 63*
*Rear: (clockwise from top left): Pen-y-Ghent; Last stretch of the*
*Pennine Way into Kirk Yetholm; On Hadrian's Wall at Walltown*
*Crags turret; View towards Crowden on the south Pennine Way*

*In memory of my parents*

'I like long walks, especially when they are taken
by people who annoy me.'

Fred Allen, American radio comedian

# Contents

# Acknowledgements

My thanks go to all those people I met during my three months 'on the road'. I hope I have done justice to those I have mentioned by name. But everyone, whose lives I briefly touched upon, helped make my journey a memorable one.

A special word of thanks must go to my two long-suffering sisters, Gill and Jenny—'Whatever is he going to get up to next?' Their support and encouragement was invaluable. Thanks also to my brothers-in-law Brian and Richard, and nieces Francesca and Samantha.

I am grateful again to Gill for her delightful drawings. Finally, I acknowledge the expertise and skill of Andy Johnson in editing my notes and breathing life into them.

# Foreword

This is an interesting account of a successful personal challenge for Tony Hobbs, and The MS Society is proud to be associated with his book.

The Society is the largest nationwide organisation dedicated to supporting the 85,000 people with MS in the UK. We provide welfare support and advice through our network of over 370 branches, national freephone helpline and respite care homes. The Society also funds 45% of all research into MS to give people hope for the future.

Land's End to John O'Groats is a challenge that makes for a fascinating story, and Tony tells it with pride.

Ken Walker
Director of Marketing
The Multiple Sclerosis Society

*Outline of the route taken*

# Introduction

I was standing at the cross-roads of life—yet again. I wanted space and time to think but I also needed a challenge. That is how I came to find myself walking from Land's End to John O'Groats. After a day's trial walk and a visit to a Millets store to buy a tent, rucksack and other equipment, I was ready. If I was to plan the thing properly I would never do it. I was off.

I had, in fact, often thought about doing the Walk, particularly after reading *Land's End to John O'Groats* by Andrew McCloy which describes three alternative routes. Other influencing factors were Dr Barbara Moore, whom I can remember back in the 1960s battling against the elements with bandaged feet; a TV play starring Joss Ackland as a senior citizen who just wanted to prove something to himself by doing the End to End; the staggering walk around the world by Ffyona Campbell; a book called *Jupiter* about a motorcyclist who toured the world; and John Muir, the amazing Scot who emigrated to the United States and disappeared into the wilderness for months on end.

It was a lovely feeling doing the walk, a feeling of being free with no worries. Every day was new and fresh. I was never really afraid or lonely. I just melded into the countryside, as though it was a perfectly natural thing to do. All my senses became more alive and I had this greater awareness of the moment and of Nature itself and I was glad to be part of it. I was passing through the very heart of Britain but by-passing all the big conurbations, travelling through areas completely new to me. And I was surprised how rural, how timeless the country was, unchanging and with so much open space.

Sometimes I was completely surrounded by wilderness for miles around. It was marvellous but awe-inspiring. One came to appreciate the vicissitudes of the weather too. The difference in being able to see exactly where I was going, and only so far as my nose. The different affects of too much sun or too much cold, and sometimes the danger of extremes. The feeling of being lost under difficult conditions was also interesting. It seemed to make me more determined. Striding along quiet lanes or over moors and mountain paths, I could shed my past cares and worries, forget my very identity and just enjoy the moment.

Meeting people was often a warm experience. Because we were strangers and would not see each other again, we could converse quite happily about anything and there would be no repercussions.

Like a tortoise I took my home with me on my back. Although my pack was heavy and at times I felt like abandoning it, it became part of me. While it slowed me down and probably doubled the amount of time I took to complete the journey, nevertheless the tent and all its contents came to be very much like a home from home. Once it was up and I had zipped the front door I could have been literally anywhere. Even the elements in the main were blotted out. I came to enjoy my night's sleep—most of the time that is, when I wasn't cold—and always woke refreshed. Again, cooking an evening meal in a billy can on my tiny stove was a thing of pleasure. I found during the day I was kept going by taking several pit-stops, and having a swig of water and a choc bar, when I was not taking photographs or writing notes. Then, sometimes at lunch-time, but mainly in the evening a visit to a local hostelry for a pint or two of real ale was very pleasurable. I came to like real ale so much I couldn't stand ordinary beer. I was a born-again drinker bent on making up for lost time.

It was also marvellous to see so many churches and other places of interest *en route* and visit towns and villages I had not seen before. In fact I spent a considerable time in sight-seeing, but then I was in no hurry. My journey covering nearly 1,200 miles was to take three months.

# 1. The First Stages

*Monday, 23rd June*

"You're mad, absolutely mad, you know that." Jenny gave vent to her feelings on the subject for the umpteenth time as we got into the car and Richard drove off.

"You'll never do it, old man," said Richard as we left the comfort of their barn conversion home in the Herefordshire countryside and set off. "You'll be lucky if you last a week."

Inwardly I agreed with my sister and brother-in-law but I didn't expect them to understand. I muttered: "Yes, well, I'll just see how it goes."

All too soon we reached Exeter and after a nice lunch, they dropped me off at St David's station. With my rucksack secured, complete with tent and sleeping mat, I waved goodbye and tottered over to the ticket office to buy a single to Penzance, the nearest rail station to my starting point. Already I felt a bit special and looked in vain for admiring glances from my fellow passengers. The three hour journey was slow and uneventful.

Arriving in Penzance, I found the bus station was next door but my bus to Land's End had left 10 minutes earlier. I checked the time-table and found the next one wasn't due for another 80 minutes. I walked around town, looking at my reflection in shop windows and relieved that I could walk reasonably well despite the weight of my rucksack.

Despite the pirate cut-outs at places like the Buccaneer and the Admiral Benbow and the car park which seemed to take up half the town, I began thinking that I should stay a few days, maybe visit St Michael's Mount or catch the ferry to the Scilly Isles. Yachts scudded by on the sparkly sea and the parish church looked splendid in its lofty position overlooking the harbour. I was still musing this over as I got back to the bus station and waited for the Land's End bus. I was still waiting quarter of an hour after it was due to have left. I checked again with the time-table. I had overlooked a microscopic diamond next to the 'Not Saturday' symbol which explained that this and the next bus did not operate until July. In effect there was no bus that evening.

I was left with three choices—walking to Land's End, catching a taxi or staying at a B & B. I felt the first was not good tactics—to walk 11 miles in the wrong direction late at night; the second was too expensive, so I went for the third. Just a few minutes walk away I found a comfortable B & B. Later that evening I lay on my bed watching TV and wondering whether my journey would ever start. To add another dimension, an item on the local news programme warned walkers in the South West to be careful of adders; already several dogs had been bitten.

## Tuesday, 24th June

I couldn't believe it. After hanging around for the equivalent of 15 hours for the Land's End bus, and waiting in a queue with 10 minutes to go, I suddenly found the key to Room No 3, which I had just vacated after consuming a very large English breakfast, was still in my pocket. I asked a woman to look after my rucksack and ran back to the guest house, thrust the key into the landlady's hand, and dashed back to the bus station. The bus came in, I clambered aboard and soon we were climbing a steep hill past Newlyn with its harbour and fishing boats, then travelling through fields of potatoes and along leafy lanes. I would enjoy walking along these, I thought. We reached Land's End and the adventure was beginning.

At the Land's End hotel, a good-looking receptionist gave me information about the Land's End - John O'Groats Association, told me to sign the book in the bar and visit the Post Room for a certificate. I made an entry in the book, too nervous to notice what other people had written, scurried out to the Last House where I got someone to take my picture and walked back over the little suspension bridge. A wailing boy was shouted at by his father, "Right that's it, we're going home. I can't stand it any more."

By the famous signpost showing that John O'Groats is 876 miles away, I had a second photo taken. Then it was on to the Post Room, where an affable young man started the certificate process. "Do you know that I jointly hold the world record," he said. "Yes, I was a member of the RAF crew which flew in a Phantom jet from John O'Groats to Land's End!" After sending cards to my sisters Jenny and Gill, I went to the Travel Office for more advice and a free ticket to the Hall of Fame of End to Enders, where I learnt about some of my predecessors such as Giovanni Ongarov who left Land's End at 6 a.m. on 20th June, 1983 on a Vincent Comet motorcycle and by 7 p.m. on 23rd June was back in Land's End. This despite freak snow and hail storms in the coldest June weather in living memory. The first person recorded as walking from End to End was the American Elihu Burritt in 1875; several nude men and women have done it on bicycles; Malcolm Edward did it pushing a pram; someone did it with a rickshaw; also cricketer Ian Botham, and Joe Lambert, the nine year-old 'diabetic dynamo' who walked from Land's End to John O'Groats in 40 days. The list is varied and long. I then enjoyed a traditional Cornish tea for lunch before finally setting off at 12.30 p.m. I had only gone a hundred yards, the car park still in sight, when a snake crossed my path. I stopped dead in my tracks and immediately thought of adders and venomous bites. The snake slithered into the undergrowth and I cautiously went on.

In his book *Land's End to John O'Groats*, whose central route I thought I would try and follow, Andrew McCloy wrote: 'whatever you do keep off the dangerous A30.' I was now on it but soon I came to a signpost marked 'Sennen Cove'. This proved to be a steep hill down to the sea at Whitesand Bay, a gorgeous sweep of sand. I asked a girl at an ice-cream van if there was a coastal path. "I don't know. I am from Sweden and only come here two weeks ago," she said.

I was going to ask again at a café at the far end of the car park, but instead stopped to look at my map, the appropriate pages from a 3 miles to the inch motoring atlas. I went to get it—the map compartment was unzipped and there was nothing inside. My heart leapt onto the beach—I had lost maps, compass, journal and route book. I had visions of going back to Land's End, even Penzance. Then it dawned on me. That morning I had transferred maps and compass to the inside compartment and there they were all safe and sound. I breathed a deep sigh of relief.

Further along the beach I climbed a steep path to some houses and a lane. I was deliberating whether to continue over the lane onto a footpath when a walker appeared. "I am German," he said in answer to my query, "but no, the footpath only goes to a farm."

So down the lane I went shortly to meet a party of walkers. "There is no path. You can't go this way," said the man, a Dutchman. I was walking back with them when another man appeared, this time a local. He advised me to take the 'German' path. Soon I found myself back on the A30.

The rucksack was getting heavier and heavier. I felt a dull ache across my shoulders and a sick feeling in my stomach. But the lane I wanted soon appeared and after a brief rest and a mouthful of water I continued on. Yellow and purple flowers were in evidence. Although the pack was heavy and my legs weary I continued on to Madron and Heamoor, where at 5.30 p.m. I located the campsite in Bone Valley. A small chatty woman ran the site and I put up my tent while she finished her supper. The camp shop was closed—the first time in 15 years, she explained—because it didn't pay.

I bought provisions at a nearby Co-op, treated myself to two pints of Ushers special at the Sportsman's Arms while writing up my notes, and returned to camp to cook supper. I'd walked between eight and ten miles that day and I felt tired. My hands seemed to have swollen a bit and my left big toe was sore. I turned in just after nine—with rain falling.

*Wednesday, 25th June*

The day rose dry, and I refreshed. After a fruit and tea breakfast I decided to try and find the Iron Age village of Chysauster. Coming to a signpost with no names I recognised, I decided to continue towards Ding Dong, drawn by its name, realising I had no idea of where I was heading. I thought that I should change my philosophy, as it doesn't matter where you're going really as long as it's roughly in the right direction. Why worry about it? Instead just enjoy the scenery. To navigate properly I should have had a proper Ordnance Survey map, but using the road map was to prove a great deal of fun. Presently I came to a sign saying New Mill and knew that Chysauster wasn't far away.

At Chysauster, a remote spot to say the least, an assistant at the English Heritage kiosk asked me questions about my journey. She and some friends had travelled along the coastal path from St Ives to Penzance and had found it tough going, very steep and, in places, over rocks. I was glad I hadn't taken that option. Rain fell as I climbed the hill to look at the nine huts or houses in this ancient settlement that was founded in about 100 A.D. and didn't survive very long.

I dawdled till the rain ceased, enjoyed a picnic lunch at a barbecue table and then moved on. I found the recommended footpath by a nearby farm but was soon lost even though the path was waymarked. I was now in an area of prickly gorse bushes and brambles, later turning into pampas grass over deep ruts creating problems for footing, and in the process soaking my boots. I struggled on towards St Erth, but almost ended up in St Ives by mistake. Off a busy road I spotted a campsite at Balnoon, and weakened.

Later that evening two young girls arrived and put up their tent near mine. They talked and giggled when I turned in at 9.30 p.m. and they continued talking and giggling into the night.

*Thursday, 26th June*

Violent winds buffeted the tent overnight and I slept fitfully. As I rose the gale was still bad and it was raining. The camp owner, a large lady, was up and about and told me "There's a low over the whole

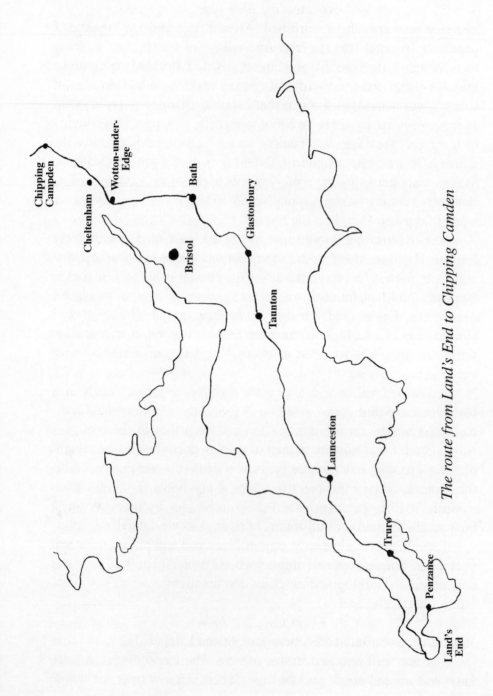

*The route from Land's End to Chipping Camden*

country and it's not expected to change until the weekend. The weather was so lovely in April and May with people sunbathing. Are you going to brave it?" I shivered. I was in two minds.

The two girls were still giggling as I decided to strike tent, a tricky operation. The wind howled and at times nearly bowled me over. Crossing the River Hayle on my way to St Erth, I was doubled up trying to prevent myself from being blown away over the causeway.

The rucksack felt very heavy and I began thinking how I could lessen the load, even considering ditching the tent and staying at B & Bs. As I pondered I saw a pig tethered in a girdle by the road, a distance from any house. I took a photo and gave the pig a piece of Mars Bar. When I reached the historic building of Godolphin House I decided, on impulse, to go in. I was greeted by a man who thought I was well wrapt for the elements and when I told him the reason for being out in them, word quickly got around. As I enjoyed a cream tea the ladies and gentlemen of the Helston branch of the RAF Benevolent Association, who were providing the teas that day, wanted to hear all about my trip and why I was going. I was a bit overwhelmed. Tony, who had met me, and his wife sat down with me and talked about their son, also in the RAF, a member of the Kinloss mountain rescue team, and his light-weight equipment—"You could do with some of that." His wife warned me of Scotland—she thought it a wasteland except for cemeteries and tumbled down buildings.

The house stays in my memory, too, notably for the dining room with its oak table, beautiful ceiling and wood panelling over the fire-place. In the King's Room, the largest and in which Charles II is supposed to have slept on his way to the Scilly Isles, I met two fasci-nating ladies. One was a spinner, very experienced, deftly feeding wool. She told me intriguing details—that the word spinster came from single women who went to different places spinning, and of the different yarns used including camel and dog. The second lady was making lace. She had a large collection of bobbins, including one made of wood from no fewer than 100 different trees, one of tung-sten aluminium and another beautifully decorated.

The Elizabethan Garden, too, was worth a visit. The gardener told me that two ponds had been discovered and a survey showed that a large area used to be planted in knot designs. It was hoped to restore the gardens to their Elizabethan splendour when ladies walked round them on raised, tree-lined paths. An exquisite honey-suckle took my eye by a garden seat. It had large tulip-shaped flowers of reddish colour with orange tips. As I left Godolphin House, the tea ladies and men wished me well and waved goodbye. It was lovely and heart-warming. Half an hour later, trudging up a steep hill, Tony and his wife, driving back to Helston, stopped and said a few words of encouragement.

Eventually I reached Porkellis and stopped at The Star to ask about campsites. While I drank a pint of Batemans, the landlord, a cheerful man from Blackheath, told me that after he had bought the pub the previous tenant had taken up squatter's rights before leaving the place in a terrible mess several months later. Everything was new including carpets throughout and a log-burning iron stove made by the local blacksmith and now spitting out embers. Two locals came in and the only campsite they knew was Caddy's Corner Farm at Carnmenellis. I drank up and hoped I would find it—I did, though it was then nearly 8 p.m. Ken, the owner, said "Rather you than me, Gunga Din," as he showed me to a field, vacant apart from rabbits and I pitched my tent in as sheltered a spot as possible. The forecast for the night was even worse. "If it gets really bad," he said, "you can use the children's playroom by the showers where there is a chair and telly." The only other people staying were in a caravan while the owner's own caravan had lost its awning to the wind. Putting up the tent was quite an achievement and after a meal of rice, dahl and cheese I got into my sleeping bag fully dressed and awaited the worst.

### Friday, 27th June

I survived the storm, sleeping pretty well despite the tent walls flap-ping. I spoke to Ken again who complained that the rabbits were taking over, eating his flowers and vegetables, and he confessed to shooting them. He also told me that there was a feud between the villagers of Carnmenellis and Penmarth because the whole area was to be called the latter.

8

The day's walk revealed verge foliage knocked about by winds in which foxgloves proliferated. I seemed to pass numerous Wesleyan churches, some converted into houses or up for sale but others still going strong. Reaching Stithians, I noticed a fish and chip shop but a woman inside changed the open sign to closed as I approached. So I trudged on thinking about lunch, eventually dipping into my supplies of cheese, rolls and water. As I approached Besso all I could think of was cream or strawberry teas. Instead there were only signs for manure or garden mulch. The day's walk ended on two miles of the busy A39 into Truro.

Finding an open fish and chip shop, I had my day's dreams of fish and chips, tea and apple pie and Cornish cream. Finding a B & B for the night, the TV news told me that Wimbledon was flooded and there had been no play for the second day, that there were floods in other parts of the country and that campers were leaving Cornwall. In the satisfying knowledge that I had completed at least 40 miles and was now off the first map page, I sank into the soft mattress under the cozy duvet and fell into a sound sleep. Not for long, however. Loud music assailed my ears. It was coming from the outer wall; the next-door neighbours were having a rave up. I had always thought Abba harmless, but I now know differently. I lay there seething for what seemed hours before the music died down and I went back to sleep.

### Saturday, 28th June

I noticed the sign in the bathroom the following morning: 'Please put toilet lid down when leaving the bathroom. In the best Chinese tradition of Feng Shui, this will ensure that all things positive and prosperous generated within this house remain in this house. Thank you. Love and light.' At breakfast Barbara, the B & B owner, apologised for the noise the previous night saying that the youngsters were usually okay, and then told me that a young couple stayed last year who were cycling from Land's End to John O'Groats on their honeymoon. "That's no way to treat your wife," I said.

I spent the morning looking round Truro, and meditated for a while in the cathedral, the first Anglican cathedral to be built since

Wren's St Paul's, until it got too noisy—preparations were being made for ordination services which were being videoed. Trying to continue my usual meditation programme, lasting over an hour twice daily, had been proving difficult. A tent, cramped and cold, was not exactly the ideal venue. My yoga exercises and the 'flying' sidhi technique, in full lotus position, were out. Additionally, the morning meditation session usually made for a late start while the evening session was hampered by tiredness and aching back. In a bookshop I came across personality key-rings with mine reading: 'Tony/Anthony from Latin Antonius. Personality with forthright and strong opinions. Usually remains calm but is explosive when roused. He is an unknown quantity.' Does that sum me up?

In the Royal Cornwall Museum I came across some oddities, notably a silver table centre piece of a camel carrying two barrels, one for tea and one for milk. When you turned a handle the camel's head would lower to fill the cups. Ingenious.

Outside in the lively shopping area, I watched members of the Cornish Potato Growers giving away free potatoes in a move to encourage supermarkets to stock Cornish potatoes alongside foreign ones. Passing Oggy Oggy, a pastry shop, I couldn't resist buying a couple of real Cornish pasties, containing, I was told, beef skirt, potatoes, swede or turnip and onion.

At about noon I eventually set off past a viaduct and on to the spotless hamlet of Idless and thence to Idless Wood, with its oak, beech, hemlock and fir, and where I enjoyed my Cornish pasties. The weather was better, the wind dying out but it was still overcast. Passing St Allen parish church, I popped in for another quiet meditation and then noticed an open bible on the altar. The following words caught my attention: 'Be on your way. And look, I am sending you like lambs among wolves. Carry no purse, or pack, and travel barefoot.'

Then I was on my way again, hopefully to Mitchell, but a five road junction had no signs. Amazingly I chose right and at long last reached Mitchell, from where there is a good view of a windfarm and I counted 15 giant wind generators. But then I went wrong, losing my way on the map and being redirected several times, only to go awry once more. Eventually I reached Summer Lodge caravan and camping site. The reception was closed but in the packed bar, a rock-band played. I had walked 12 to 15 miles in 10 hours, with a brief stop for crisps and a pint.

### Sunday, 29th June

It started raining as I dismantled the tent, then it poured down, so I didn't leave until 12.30 after a lazy breakfast in the camp café. Still pondering on ways to lighten my rucksack, I eventually came to Castle-an-Dinas, an Iron Age fortress overlooking trade routes and, like many, with supposed links with King Arthur. It was still pouring with rain and I got soaked, including some of my gear as I found later. Walking into Withiel I met a couple on a tandem. They were curious to know about my walk as they had cycled from John O'Groats to Woking and were now, after a break, completing the journey. They enjoyed walking, too, and would like to walk the End to End but haven't the time. This was their second tandem; apparently bits always kept falling off their first one. Further on I passed a cottage with four army vehicles inside the front gate. On the other side were 11 more vehicles, including jeeps, lorries, armoured personnel carriers and even a riverboat, all with desert warfare camouflage. On the gate was a skull and crossbones and a 'Keep Out' sign. Finally I reached Ruthern Valley campsite, having walked about 12 miles in 7 and a half hours. I was surprised at the price, but I was told by the owner's wife, pleasantly but firmly, that it was the going rate and in July prices would be going up.

After erecting my tent, I phoned Jenny. "I was hoping it would be you. I've been very worried, thinking of you in this awful weather. We've had the central heating on, it's been so cold." She had heard of a 20 year-old also doing the walk who had had difficulties before getting support and then walking without a pack. Why couldn't I do the same? I then cooked my usual campsite supper of rice, dahl, ginger and vegetable soup on the stove inside my tent, plus beer and ice cream bought from the camp shop. I thought I should try and keep to my vegetarian diet, but it was proving difficult what with the temptation of English breakfasts at B & Bs, and pub meals. I tried to sleep at 10.30 p.m. but young late night revellers with lots of laughing made it difficult.

## Monday, 30th June

I rose early for a change, but then dozed off after a tent breakfast, making for a late start once again. From the camp owner I learnt about Mad Mike McGuire, whose hobby was to buy old military vehicles and do them up. All his vehicles were in working order, and he loved talking about them and letting children have rides.

Today I was taking the nine mile Camel trail to Poley's Bridge, created out of a disused railway track. It was generally a quiet walk, partly through gnarled, twisted trees with fresh green leaves, except for several cyclists and a party of schoolchildren. I noticed a sign on a farm gate: 'Beware of the bull - survivors will be prosecuted or trespassers allowed in free. Bull will charge later. Steve, farmer.' As I approached the long, sprawling village of Poley's Bridge I noticed chimney smoke through the now drizzly weather, but, unbelievably, no café—it closed down three years ago. Nevertheless, a local shop meant I could buy some provisions. During the afternoon I thought "Why am I doing this walk?" As a penance, a need for my own space and time to think things over, a need to meet people and behave naturally? I certainly feel freer to talk because I don't know them and won't see them again. I hope perhaps to brighten their lives a little, too.

Pressing on towards Bodmin Moor, I meant to seek permission to camp at a farm, but on the edge of the moor at St Breward it seemed very cold, wet, remote, bleak and it was getting dark. I chickened out as soon as I saw a farm B & B sign. I declined the farmer's offer to take me to the pub for a meal, but his wife gave me biscuits and home-made cake.

## Tuesday, 1st July

The day started with a huge breakfast—two sausages, two slices of bacon, two eggs, mushrooms and tomatoes, plus three giant pieces of toast, cornflakes, tea and orange juice. Even so, I set off relatively early for once—just before 10 a.m.

Once again it was raining hard as I headed towards Camelford. As I walked along the B3266 I noticed smears on my anorak pockets and trousers; I later realised it was rain washing off the sealant I had applied. I decided not to head across the moor, but kept taking wrong turns at unmarked junctions, even finding myself walking westwards at one stage; back on course, I came to a crossroads with a cream tea sign. Irresistible. And I thought it was on the right road too. After walking for at least a further mile I came to what proved to be a farm-house, walked through the deserted car park and found the café closed. I banged on the door. An old woman, probably in her 90s, her grey hair in a bun, answered the door. She explained that her daughter, who ran the café, was out picking up her children from school, but added: "I'll make tea for ye—I know what it's like on Moor. We've had no summer this year."

She invited me into the kitchen and I sat at the large kitchen table while she prepared the cream tea. I was soon joined by a couple with an 18 month old grandchild. The old lady told me how to get to St Clether, but I knew better of course and continued on down the road to find myself in Rough Tor car park. With my tail between my legs I retraced my steps, wasting an hour and adding a further two miles. Eventually I came to Crowdy Reservoir, which I thought I had passed ages ago, and after seeing a sign which read 'Pissing Place' reached a disused airfield. It took me an hour to cross this and then I needed to find a campsite. On reaching a farm I thought about enquiring about camping, but walked past, saw a campsite sign and went back. The place was deserted, but I found a field with a loo and running water. I promptly used the loo—the flush worked and it even had loo paper. I pitched my tent by some trees, in a pleasant and comfy spot. There was a fragrant smell from lush grass, soon replaced by a rather different smell as I took off my boots and outer socks. My feet were beginning to show signs of wear with blisters and bruises.

Once again it rained most of the night, and I was thankful for a decent sleeping bag.

*Wednesday, 2nd July*

I surprised myself and was away by 9.45 a.m., reaching St Clether in just over an hour, as the rain eased off. I spent an hour in the church and visiting the holy well and earlier chapel, half a mile away. St Clether is named after Cleder or Clederus, one of 24 children from Wales who came to Cornwall in the 6th century. He chose the site of a spring in Inner Valley to build his hermitage. As I plodded on I realised I was getting disillusioned, making slow progress and with such a heavy pack. In addition the rain came heavily on once more. I determined to try and make Launceston so as to feel I was making headway, even though that meant some time on the dreaded A30 being sprayed by cars and lorries.

By 4.30 I was sitting in the Mad Hatters' Tea Shop tasting Mad Hatters' tea, a light spicy brew, the recipe of which only the owner knows and she will take it with her when she dies, or so she told me. I also enjoyed a Cornish cream tea plus a pavlova. The owner also told me she had opened the shop about two and a half years previously, after suddenly coming up with the idea. "I must have been barmy," she added.

I started to feel better, though still aching, especially in the shoulders. The last stretch was really bad with my right shoulder making me feel sick—I would have to sort something out. I walked around Launceston disconsolately till eventually a postman pointed me to a B & B near the only remaining gateway to the old walled town. The B & B turned out to be run by an Indian family, so I also decided on a hot curry at a local Indian restaurant. Later on I phoned Gill who reassured me that it would have been worse if I had started in Scotland as the weather there was even more atrocious. My brother-in-law, Brian said: "Take your time, mate. Go at your own speed."

I thought I was, for I had been walking for nine days and had completed just 100 miles. Richard, my other brother-in-law, had bet me I wouldn't get this far. Pity I didn't have the courage of my convictions and put a bet on myself.

# 2. The Next Hundred Miles

*Thursday, 3rd July*

Once again I woke feeling refreshed and ready to continue. Breakfast was shared with two middle-aged female American tourists from Michigan. One, with close cropped iron grey hair, said: "When you Brits kept on about the weather I knew there was something seriously wrong."

Sadly, I decided to get rid of my sleeping bag, to lighten my load, as well as turfing out every non-essential item. I posted the sleeping bag to my sister, Jenny, and stocked up with supplies. Then, in the drizzle, I visited Launceston Castle, or rather its remains, and the church, where a milk urn was used as a money box because of the number of burglaries at nearby churches.

Leaving Launceston just after midday, I took the A388 to Dutson and then continued over a 15th century stone bridge to St Giles on the Heath. I celebrated my entry into Devon with a somewhat unspectacular lunch of bun, cheese, banana, plums and water, taken, as often in the rain, in a bus shelter. The afternoon progress was good, made better by the sun coming out and the anorak off. I made Northlew my target and progress continued well, partly due to better signposting—well done Devon. Spirits definitely more buoyant today. Reaching Northlew I went straight to the Green Dragon for a pint of Courage Best and a packet of crisps. The landlady phoned a local farm and sorted out my night's campsite. We were joined by a pretty fair-haired girl, wearing a bomber jacket and baseball cap, and a boy whom she promptly cuffed round the ear, adding "Sit down and be quiet." Over a beer and a cigarette, she chatted to the landlady.

"I'm having a foster brother—neat isn't it. Look, this is the charm necklace I was given for my 21st birthday." In response to a couple of questions from the landlady, she added "Yes, I'm still working at the pig farm, but I haven't been doing much archery lately."

Over a second pint, one always seemed too few, I brought up the subject of Gordon Brown's recent budget. The landlady said it was supposed to be a people's budget, but she didn't know what people. The girl said she might have to give up smoking with cigarettes going up. She then talked about pig farms and that the best way to kill pigs was to "tramp on them". The landlady and myself both agreed it was a good thing we hadn't had bacon for breakfast.

"I'll break your fingers if you misbehave," the girl snapped at the boy, who had been making a noise.

"You wouldn't," said the landlady.

"I would." The girl then brought something from a pocket. "This is my lucky 27 tag; I pulled it off a cow's ear."

As I left, the landlady showed me how to get to Lower Crowden Farm and asked me to send her a postcard from John O'Groats. As ever I knew better and went the wrong way, once again retracing my steps to find the farm.

### Friday, 4th July

I had a rotten night, being unable to sleep because of the cold. To start with I stripped and lay in a bed liner and survival bag with anorak over. Nearby there was a loud noise of a stream, the sudden plopping sound as of fish, and occasional animal noise. I think I also disturbed some cows with the crackling noise of the plastic survival bag. I was too cold and couldn't settle, so I put on trousers, shirt, sweater, anorak and gloves. It was still no good. Took off the survival bag, which was wet inside and felt cold, and put on outer trousers and socks. It didn't seem long before I heard the dawn chorus and I slumbered fitfully until 8 a.m. A hot shower helped revive me. Over breakfast I read the *Cornish and Devon Post*. One story took my particular fancy: 'On May 24 to June 1, Launceston town councillor, Mr Ron Treen, 65, (he had his birthday during the walk) and about 40 other walkers undertook the mammoth task of walking from The Lizard, Cornwall to Blackheath, London. The walk was to commemorate the 500th anniversary of the Cornish uprising. Mr Treen had a triple heart bypass 10 years ago.'

I still felt a bit jaded and washed out after last night, but presently reached Hatherleigh. Having looked at the church which dates back to Saxon days, though the main part was built in the 14th and 15th centuries, I looked round the town, which I liked, with its life-like statue of three farmers looking at some sheep, its hotel, three pubs and tea-room, in which I soon found myself. The tea-lady said she had met a 60 year-old man last year who was completing the John O'Groats to Land's End walk, whose only trouble was in Glastonbury where he had his wallet stolen while camping. She hoped I got to John O'Groats all right. An hour further on I reached Monkokehampton, where I had a Devonshire farmhouse ice-cream from the Post Office which was run by two 70 year-olds. Later I came to Bondleigh, meaning I'd covered about 13 miles. I decided to keep up the good progress and aim for Zeal Monachorum, but ran out of luck, took a wrong turning, and retraced my steps. Sitting at a crossroads trying to work out where Zeal was, a farmer came up one road, driving a brown and white cow before him. He shouted to me to stop it. I tried but it ran past and out of sight. Then it came back again, chased by a Land Rover, but at the junction it squeezed past and bolted along the road to Zeal, as I was conveniently told.

"It's a wild one," said the farmer, who had a florid face and a large stomach. As I walked on to Zeal the Land Rover reappeared and overtook me, carrying the farmer. Subsequently I passed the farmer and driver looking at tracks in a field. A man on a tractor cutting the grass shouted to me that the "cow was on top field" and he passed on the good news to the others.

Arriving in Bow I asked a man I spotted gardening if there was a campsite and was told there was one just past the nearby Dutch barn. Sure enough there it was, but private—members of the Caravanning and Camping Club only. I tried reception at a bungalow, but there was no-one there. I was just starting to walk disconsolately away, when a car drove up and a young man said "I think we might find room for you, I know what it's like." His parents were away and I could stay free of charge. I calculated I'd walked about 19 miles in 10 hours, but my feet were in a bad state, with plenty of blisters. I chucked out the sheep's wool I'd been wrapping around my feet as it was smelling something awful.

### *Saturday, 5th July*

I needed to sleep with all clothes on again. As I was leaving camp, a stoutish lady in one of the caravans asked me if I enjoyed the walk. "It's like purgatory" I replied.

I passed through Zeal Monachorum as there was nothing there and beyond noticed a sign 'Danger - keep out. Wild birds'—then spotted them, a herd of ostriches, of which two came up to the gate. The friendliest were of a light brown colour; those of a dark brown were more aloof. Reaching Down St Mary I made a 40 minute detour to a vineyard, but found it closed till later in the day. I took lunch in a bus shelter again, though it was sunny today, and subsequently saw the Sturt Arms, which I couldn't resist, especially as it had its own ale.

Paths took me out into Morchard Bishop, after walking through fields of cows, wheat and sheep, and where I found a tea shop. In the afternoon I caught up with a flock of sheep being moved to new pasture. When the farmer found out where I was going, he gave me a bottle of Lucosade—a nice gesture—and wished me well.

Later I came to a farm where I met an old farmer leaning against the gate and we started talking about his Jersey cows. His name was Aubrey. He had pure snow white hair under his hat and was probably in his 80s, even 90s. He offered me a drink and soon I was enjoying a mug of delicious fresh Jersey milk. Aubrey told me he had retired and sold the herd when he was 70, but then bought back a few at £40 a head over his selling price. He'd given up his milk quota, so now fed the milk to the pigs—he needed some reason to get out of the

18

house, for his wife has Altzheimer's disease. When he sat with her in her bedroom she didn't recognise him, saying: "There's Aubrey out in the field cutting the grass." There was nothing anyone could do about the disease; but he could cope by having something to do every day and had good memories. His eyes were lively and he spoke in a soft Devon burr.

"The only dumb animals are the two legged kind," he said. He gave an example of a sick sheep which dragged itself to the side of a field under some trees, and so gained protection from the next day's snow-storm, and another of a cow which protected him and his daughter against a stampeding herd set off by a rogue heifer. He gave me another mug of milk and invited me to camp on his land, but we had gone through so many options it had become confusing, and as I didn't want to take advantage, I made my goodbyes and continued on towards Bickleigh. At about 8 p.m. I spotted an enticing field where a crop had just been cut, and decided to give it a go. I erected the tent, cooked supper, and put a special plastic skin on my blisters. The evening was beautifully calm and serene, the only noise being a tractor driving up and down a nearby field.

### Sunday, 6th July

After refilling my water bottles at a farm that I found, I rambled through Cadeleigh and into Bickleigh. It sits by the River Exe over which there is a lovely old stone bridge, and is full of posh hotels and pubs. While sitting by the church looking at my map, a voice said: "You are not looking lost are you?" It was an old man, tall, straight, in the 70 to 80 age range, wearing Wellingtons and carrying a stick. He told me he used to walk 20 miles a day when ploughing by horse, and then went dancing in the evening. He had lived within a 20 mile radius of Bickleigh all his life, and used to know everyone in the village, though not any more. We chatted about BSE. He said that the meat, instead of being burnt, should be sent to the starving.

After parting I headed towards Cullompton. By lunch time I had reached Butterleigh where I found the delightful Butterleigh Inn. I downed a pint of Cotleigh Barn Owl, followed by one of Tawny

Bitter. Both were excellent, and were accompanied by a large lunch topped off with special bread pudding with clotted cream.

The afternoon walk was through woodland, and past huge yew trees and tall oaks. I reached Cullompton in the late afternoon and visited the church which 'is unique throughout England, and possibly Christendom, in possessing the original carved wooden base of the mediaeval rood. It is sometimes called the Golgotha because it is carved with skulls and rocks and crossbones - the more vividly to bring home to the eye, and thence to the heart, that it was among condemned criminals and sinners and "with the wicked that He made His grave."' It must be at least 500 years old. I had arrived at the church just as a young man, who turned out to be the curate, unlocked the door and enquired: "Are you from the guided walk group?" Later, the group, respectable people of all ages including a boy in a wheelchair, came in. The church had a glorious wagon roof in the nave, which reminded me of St David's Cathedral in Wales. The Golgotha is two massive pieces of oak, carved to represent rocks covered with skulls and bones and you can see the socket for the cross and the platform for Mary and John. It originally stood on top of the screen and was probably removed in the time of Edward VI.

Cullompton itself has a broad, long High Street with plenty of shops, including a laundrette which I should have used, hotels and pubs, though the latter mostly advertised Karaoke and had loud music blaring out. I pressed on to Uffculme where I found a Caravan Camp sign for members only by the river and a hump-back bridge, but a tall, white haired lady let me stay in a nice, quiet spot by the stream, away from the caravanners.

### Monday, 7th July

Another cold night, so only fitful sleep, but it dawned bright and beckoned a lovely day. My route led by the River Culm where I walked a short way with a young pregnant woman and her young son. She told me the area was subject to flooding, and to watch out for the cows—sometimes they chased you. When I came to a herd they seemed docile enough. Coming to a bridge I spoke to a nice old lady who said she knew someone who had just done the Land's End to John O'Groats journey on a 1946 Velocette motor bike despite three heart by-pass operations. Continuing on by the river I came to a field with heifers. They were curious and when I shouted my magic word "hut" a few times, they stood back respectfully. Over a deep muddy style I met more heifers, looking even more interested and coming straight at me. I shouted "hut", "hut" and they left me alone.

I continued along an old, disused, and overgrown light railway track into Culmstock where I stocked up with supplies. For once I eschewed the possible pub, and had my lunch on a seat by the ceno-taph. Then it was on to Woodgate and the beacon. How do you manage to miss a beacon and a 175 ft tall monument? Quite easily. I kept on towards a TV transmitter mast along a wide bridleway, then through woods where I met an old gentleman and his male friend walking their dogs. They told me that I had missed the beacon (it was behind me) but that the monument was only a mile away. I could soon see the monument in the distance, came to a junction with no sign, left a cow in charge of my pack, sighted Wellington again, retrieved my pack and continued along the Taunton road. I then decided to go down a lane which turned into a quagmire of cows' muck, practically up to my knees. I climbed a style, thought better of it, and retraced my steps, sloshing through the muck. I was back on the road to Wellington, I thought, when the old gentleman, now driving a car, stopped and told me that the entrance was on a different road. Back I went again. I still couldn't see an entrance, so I went in through a field of parked trailers, underneath an electric fence, through a field of cows and finally reached the monument. It was built in 1892 in memory of the Duke and is impressive, with views to the village of Wellington, from which he took his name. I chatted to a young man and his girl friend who had been necking by the monument. After he heard about my walk, the man said he now felt unfit. He got up at three every day to milk the cows, but he loved the stuff cold and said in the summer he drank as much as went into the lorry. The girl came from Wellington and said she had walked 18 miles in six hours one day but didn't fancy walking any greater distance. When I left the young couple were necking in the car.

*En route* to Taunton I passed into Somerset. Taunton itself seemed a long time coming. Entering the town centre, I was approached by a dark-looking woman and two boys who said they couldn't get a single room anywhere. Later, as I sat on a bench in the shopping centre, a youth with a bag came up and said the woman, his mother, had sent him. There was a B & B opposite C & A but no singles, but he would pay £15 if I shared a room with him, he would even sleep on the floor. I said I didn't really want to share. His bag started shaking and he opened it—inside were two puppies. "Staffs," he called them and said they were four weeks old. The woman and the other two boys now turned up. I again declined the room share, and thankfully they went off towards the railway.

An hour later I finally found a reasonably priced room in a B & B. I noted I was getting thinner, and that my face and arms were at last sunburnt.

## Tuesday, 8th July

How much easier it is to meditate in a quiet, warm and comfortable bedroom. I could do my asanas and also a limited 'flying', or hopping—I hope I never damaged the bed springs! At breakfast a plump and middle-aged woman said her mother's uncle had been the first, or one of the first, to go from Land's End to John O'Groats by motorcycle, about 100 years ago. She didn't know how he managed about petrol stations, as there were hardly any in Cornwall even nowadays.

After breakfast I first went to Millets, where four girl assistants and a visiting commercial director helped me sort out a chest strap for my rucksack and advised on weight distribution. I visited St Magdalene Church where I spoke to a man in a black cassock, with pointed nose and chin, who said they had a Green Man, showing me a photo of the face and also pointing to the ceiling where it could just be seen. He also said that one of the angels with a dog in the magnificent ceiling had the sort of facial expression which showed she had had a bad night. He mentioned that a survey by Canterbury Cathedral revealed that today's youth wanted 'a feeling of spirituality', and for his part was playing plain music in the church. When a girl came in to play the organ, he went to turn the music off. "She's a natural, off to Queen's College," he added.

In the afternoon I left Taunton and walked along the river to Creech St Michael. It was very hot again, so I stopped at the Ruiston Arms and enjoyed a pint of Butcombe bitter and a cheese sandwich. I spent the afternoon walking along the river Tone through the Somerset Levels, the last part a jungle of nettles. When I reached North Curry I was surprised to find the local shop still open, with an old man of at least 80 serving two boys. Further on I came to Jays Nest, a tea-house, where the lady took pity on me and, despite being closed, opened up and offered me refreshment. She, an ex-PT teacher, and her husband, a stockbroker, decided to pack it in and come to Stoke St Gregory, which I had now reached. Last summer, an elderly couple, in their 70s, stayed the night whilst undertaking the Land's End to John O'Groats walk. She mentioned there was a campsite on the far side of the village, and there I went, and tried out the new Polarshield blanket I had bought that morning at Millets.

### Wednesday, 9th July

The morning's walk lay along the River Parrett, then through fields of cows and corn. I had to move on a small herd of heifers blocking a style over which I wanted to climb. Langport was reached at lunchtime and I headed for the Langport Arms Hotel. Vegetable lasagna was off, as was scampi and haddock, so I settled for spicy tiger prawns and chips together with a pint of Our Ken real ale from the Cottage Brewery. The room was full of different characters. At the bar a sunburnt man was with an old fellow, thin as a rake, with dangling arms and a bent back. "We go back a long time," said the sunburnt man. They discussed crime and prisons, and how expensive they were. The old man was quiet with rheumy eyes. A group of five ladies were having lunch and seemed as if they had come straight from a Women's Institute meeting. One, with a loud, schoolmarmish voice, said she had heard on the radio about a flower 45,000 years old. "What is so special about that. An amoeba is millions of years old, and I go back to Adam."

I conveniently reached Somerton at tea time to find the Buttercross tea-room which served a cream tea I just couldn't resist. That was followed by the benches outside the Castlebrook Inn at Compton Dundon. Here I fell into conversation with the landlord, who had run a variety of pubs in London and Kent. He told one story where he heard a rumpus out the back of the pub and found a man with his head in the urinal, and blood everywhere. His throat had been cut. He was a drug pusher and had been killed by a man who used the pub regularly.

I stayed the night at a campsite three miles short of Glastonbury.

*Thursday, 10th July*

Today was just going to be a short stroll to Glastonbury, using the rest of the day to explore the town and its environs. Indeed I could see Glastonbury Tor from just the other side of the farmhouse. The tower is all that is left of Church of St Michael, and that became my first target once I'd sorted out a B & B.

There is a steep zig zag path to the top, and notices tell of all kinds of fact and fantasy, that the church was originally founded in the 5th or 6th century A.D. but the second chapel on the Tor was apparently built after a destructive earthquake of 1275; that the terraces (strip lynchets or mediaeval fields) formed a 3D maze; of a secret entrance to the underworld; that the Tor was the scene of the hanging, drawing and quartering of Richard Whiting, last Abbot of Glastonbury, when Henry VIII dissolved the abbey in 1539. A topographic marker pointed out that Cadbury Castle, reputedly Camelot, was 11 miles distant.

I took a different route down and visited Chalice Well, its source somewhere deep under the Mendip Hills. The well itself is capped by a wrought iron lid with a design of interlocking circles, but the water with its high iron content can be tasted at the nearby Lion's Head drinking area. While I was sampling the water, a young robin, feathers still fluffy, bob-bobbed along up to and under my seat. I kept perfectly still.

It was then the turn of the abbey set in its 33 acres of gardens. The abbot's kitchen stands separately and is roofed with a tiered

24

spire. It used to have four fires, the smoke from which left through a lantern in the very high ceiling. There were cauldrons which could cook soup, meat, eggs and puddings at the same time. I was amazed at the size of the church, 580 ft long compared with Canterbury Cathedral's 547 ft, and its central tower was 217 ft high compared to Canterbury's 235 ft. Inside the church ruins is the site of King Arthur's tomb. A plaque read: 'In the year 1191 the bodies of King Arthur and his Queen were said to have been found on the south side of the Lady Chapel. On 19th April 1278 their remains were removed in the presence of King Edward I and Queen Eleanor to a black marble tomb on this site. This tomb survived until the dissolution of the abbey in 1539.' I also saw the thorn tree in abbey grounds, next to St Patrick's Chapel, which is said to have sprung from the staff of Joseph of Arimathea, the Virgin Mary's uncle and a disciple of Jesus. A wealthy trader, he may have come on an earlier visit with Jesus to obtain tin. 'But he definitely came in 37 A.D. bringing, so it is said, the Holy Grail, containing Christ's blood, and legend has it on Wearyall Hill he rested his staff which became a thorn tree. He also brought with him the chalice and started the Christian church in this country.' The tree blossoms at Christmas and is the first of the thorn trees in Glastonbury. Another famous saint connected with Glastonbury is St Dunstan who was abbot before going to Canterbury. St Patrick also visited.

There were lots of tourists, but somehow I felt lonely as I didn't get a very warm response when trying to talk to some of them. Neither did I feel anything special about either the Tor or the abbey, no sudden mystical revelations, but then should I have done? In addition, the tandoori restaurant I chose for the evening meal was not very friendly.

### *Friday, 11th July*

Availed myself of the laundrette in town before setting off, and whilst waiting, visited the church of St John the Baptist. Refreshments were being served and gifts sold in the south aisle, whilst a small service was being conducted in the Chapel of St Nicholas. I was happy to see all this activity. In the south aisle were two large carvings by Ernest Blensdorf, of German origin, both in elm, one of the Madonna and Child, the other of the Resurrection. Abbot Dunstan probably had the first church built, but it was rebuilt 500 years ago. One of the Glastonbury thorn trees is in the grounds. Time also allowed a visit to the Lake Village museum above the tourist office. 2,000 years ago much of Somerset's landscape was covered by a marshy sea in which lake villages were constructed, one of which was discovered by Arthur Bulleid, a local amateur archae- ologist, at the end of the last century. This particular settlement was used between 150 B.C. and 50 A.D., and had a maximum of 18 houses and 200 people.

In wandering around the town, I noticed several men with tattoos and Mohican hair cuts and women with lots of beads and shawls. I didn't really feel any rapport with anyone.

Collecting my washing and rucksack, I set off along the old Wells road to the A34 and then down a lane past Hartlake Bridge to North Wootton. The Tor stood out beautifully. The afternoon's walk was along direct, straight and narrow lanes, with ditches on either side full of green water, beyond which were fields full of brown and white cows and heifers. At one point the road was blocked by cows and I recalled Thomas Gray's 'Elegy Written in a Country Churchyard':

> The Curfew tolls the knell of parting day,
> The lowing herd wind slowly o'er the lea,
> The ploughman homeward plods his weary way,
> And leaves the world to darkness and to me.

In mid-afternoon I stopped at Wootton vineyard, where the owner, a Mrs. Gillespie, appeared. "Do you do sampling?" I asked.

"If people come to buy. It doesn't look as if you could carry much."

"I'll buy a bottle," I said.

"Come along then." I tried a chilled dry white wine, then a fruity one like an Alsace. She also gave me a small glass of fiery tasting Eau de Vie. Apparently vineyards were recorded locally in the Domesday Book and there is a 13th century carving in Wells Cathedral of the Grape Stealers. She and her husband had not originally intended to grow grapes but conditions were ideal with the right soil, south facing ground and good weather. This year was not so good, she said. Early fine weather in April had brought the grapes on and then in May there was frost and 80% were lost.

In the village of Croscombe a voice cried: "Do you want a drink?" I turned and saw an old man standing in the doorway of a cottage. "I knew you weren't a youngster and you were puffing a bit," he said. "Come in. Have a drink, whatever you like." I took water from the tap and filled my bottle. Funnily enough, I had been thinking about getting water for the night and had tried unsuccessfully to buy some at the shop. The old man was in his late 70s, tall and big. "Stay awhile and rest," he said. I sat myself down, and after a chat about Australia, which he had visited three times, I excused myself and he came outside and walked with me. His left leg was paralysed, caused by a stroke, and he had an invalid's vehicle. As we went up the hill, he pointed out flowers and plants—wild strawberry, "stinker" with small violet flowers, "cheese and bread" ("we used to eat it"), and sloeberry. He continued to reminisce. "Over there we picked mushrooms, that field swarmed with rabbits. Back there used to be a silk farm and a factory. On this lane, horses used to drag logs—there's too much traffic now. Over there was a donkey farm, but they made too much noise and it got closed down." We had reached the new church cemetery which only had two graves. "My wife died of cancer, I'm all alone," he said. A car stopped and offered him a lift.

I waved him goodbye and then plodded on to a campsite which I was recommended by a passing farmer. After I'd erected my tent I tried to meditate but found it difficult after a day's walk with all the aches and pains. Or was it the thought of the wine—Wootton's Schonburger, medium dry English table wine. I sipped it while cooking rice, dahl, ginger and Batchelors soup, but it was not quite so good warm! For sweet I had dates, raisins and apricots—cooked with wine. As I drank more, I got rather maudlin and wondered what I was doing there.

### Saturday, 12th July

Felt a bit hung over as I packed up in a misty morning. A herd of cows went by, all with very big udders, ready for milking. As the mist started to lift I began the walk into Bath, all along roads, the last part along the A367. It became a hot day for walking, and as soon as I reached the town I looked for the first 'vacant' sign outside a B & B, and took their last remaining room.

I was often asked whether I was lonely on my walk. Not usually, but that night I did feel in need of companionship. As it had started to rain I did not linger in town, but when I got back to the B & B, there was no one in the lounge so, despite my feelings, I went straight to my bedroom, a small attic room. Here I calculated that I had now covered over 210 miles—but there was still a long way to go.

# 3. The Cotswold Way

*Sunday, 13th July*

The next part of the journey would be along the Cotswold Way, so the first need was to buy a guide in town. But in the centre of Bath I was distracted by a boule competition in Queen Square. A tall, good-looking blonde girl told me it was an annual competition run over a weekend. Yesterday had been for professional players, today was the turn of restaurateurs, and so more relaxed. The event had been started some years previously by the French owner of The Beaujolais restaurant, and it had grown to the point where up to 100 teams took part with some 20 games going on at any one time. A lot of people were playing boule on a specially laid out and sanded path running round the park amidst trees and marquees. "It gets quite serious," the girl added. "Once when I was scoring I took the wrong score, they throw them at you very fast, and we had to re-run the game." She was scorer for her team from the Frances Hotel across the road. "I'm too fond of my comforts to want to do that," she said after I told her of my walk.

I found a Waterstones and a guide, before sampling their upstairs café. I promptly spilt a jug of cream, thinking it was one of those cartons, and there was cream everywhere. "Glad it happens to somebody else," said a lady.

I left Bath via the Crescent and the Royal Victoria Gardens, joining the Cotswold Way at Penn Hill Road. I would be on this Way

29

for the next 100 miles amidst rolling limestone hills to Chipping Camden. The route involved many beautiful views over Bath, of tile roofs and stone buildings, gradually retreating into the distance. Even the new estates seem to be in crescents. A party of walkers in shorts passed, one saying "Nice to see a professional out." I gave a maniacal laugh, but felt good. At times I wasn't quite sure where I was for the guide was too detailed to follow all the time. At one point I passed a memorial to 'Sarah Louise Gray died here 17-11-95 - aged 17.' It was in a lovely spot overlooking Bath and I wondered who she was and how she died. As I rose up onto the crest of the hills I gained a view across Bristol and the Severn Valley with the towers of the Severn Bridge across to the hills of Wales. I came to another monument, this time to Sir Bevil Grenville, killed during the Civil War battle at nearby Lansdown Hill, fought on 5th July 1643. The 25ft high monument is topped by a griffin crest of the Grenville or Granville family.

As the afternoon wore on I got directions to Cold Ashton from a young American girl on a mountain bike, after thinking I was getting lost, for I was only picking up yellow public footpath signs. Ye of little faith, for I soon came to a CW sign—I had been on the right track all the time. I reached Cold Ashton just before 6 p.m., but the White Hart was not yet open. I decided to carry on across a field of young broad beans (tasted delicious) to Pennsylvania, where the Swan Inn was also closed. Then, after nearly being run over by a lorry as I crossed the A46, it was on through Dyrham Wood, but it was gloomy as it had started to rain. I passed through the village of Dyrham, and then past the entrance to Dyrham House, which looked beautiful, and on towards Tormarton looking for a convenient place to pitch the tent. I noticed several patches in the grass which looked like places where someone else had camped, and chose one of these for myself.

My feet felt not so bad today, having walked on hardly any tarmac—it does make a difference. Though there was a rural scene from my tent, the traffic from the nearby M4 made a continual noise.

## Monday, 14th July

This was to be a day of dogs and cows. A little white dog tried to get in my tent as I was getting up, but its owner, a man in shorts and boots, appeared together with another dog, this one small and brown. He didn't seem to think my being there unusual. I had to be careful how I walked, for there were snails and lots of little grey slug things, some on their own, some together, mating. About 10 in the morning I reached a picnic area off the A46 where I tried the toilet but it was in an awful state and there was no loo paper. At the nearby café the assistant said she wasn't able to give me any tap water—couldn't even serve it with orange squash, it had to be bottled. "New regulations out last year."

Once over the motorway I was soon in Tormarton, where I paused to look at the parish church. Lunch was taken at the Dog Inn, Old Sodbury, which served Bob's, a local real ale, a nice, mellow drop not too strong. I also visited the church here and noticed, coming into the graveyard from the pub, a grave to Duncan Ramsey, who died on 19th June 1987, aged 11, which had fresh flowers. The church had an unusual pig and mouse carving, and an old hand bier, presented in 1902. During the afternoon I passed through Sodbury hillfort, a big circular fortification stretching over 11 acres. Originally constructed in the Iron Age, it was also used by the Romans and then the Saxons. But on leaving the hillfort, I lost my way a couple of times, found gates and styles surrounded by a sea of mud, and had to be wary of cattle. Crossing one long pasture, a heifer resting its head on the back of another suddenly got up and headed towards me. It had horns. I cried "hut"—the magic formula—and it stopped dead in its tracks. Then I went through Frith Wood; nature called, and I used my trowel for the first time, by a tree. It was particularly muddy underfoot and impassable by a gate so I climbed over barbed wire, and the pack got caught. Then crossing another field, a pack of black and white cows turned towards me. "Hut, hut" I cried. It stopped them but still they advanced every time I moved. This time I was a bit worried, as there was a hedge to one side and the gate was a long way off. I picked up a stick and shouted again. Eventually they stopped and I was able to continue, albeit with fearful looks behind.

While I was resting a bit later, they all came flying by at quite a speed and passed out of sight.

In the late afternoon I reached the village of Hawkesbury Upton and visited the Somerset monument which stands 650ft high in honour of General Lord Robert Somerset, who served under Wellington at Waterloo. There is a balcony—144 steps up—but it was closed. As the afternoon turned into evening, I was finding it difficult to locate a suitable site; I thought sheep and cattle were better provided for. Eventually I found a level, tall grassy plot just off the track and erected the tent, spotting a big tear in the tent bag from the barbed wire altercation. I seemed to have spent about 10 hours on the go and only progressed 13 miles. What had I been doing? I suppose having to climb over lots of styles, opening gates and avoiding mud all slows one down. As I was pondering on this, there was a commotion at the front of the tent. I opened the flap and a young Great Dane tried to burst in. Before going to sleep an elderly woman and a man came back with the dog. "It will have to come down", I heard one say. I hoped they weren't referring to the tent.

### Tuesday, 15th July

Today was the start of my third week out from Land's End. I woke to find little slugs in the tent, and shortly after setting off lots of tiny frogs, small as a finger nail.

The day proved frustrating in that I was constantly lost and retracing my steps. After passing through Alderley, a rather quiet and smart looking village, I headed down Kennerwell Lane, another of those long paths probably used by sheep drovers and completely covered by overhead trees. But then I spotted a yellow arrow leading over a style and, congratulating myself on being sharp eyed, over the style I went. It was, of course, a path that met the CW, not the CW itself. After much retracing of ground, and of asking directions, I eventually rejoined the long distance path and at last reached Wotton-under-Edge. Here I visited the Perry and Dawes almshouses and chapel, a gift in 1630 of Hugh Perry and extended through the bequest of Thomas Dawes in 1711. A lunch in the town's Coffee House included fruit pie and ice-cream. Suitably refreshed, I visited the 700 year-old parish church of St Mary the Virgin, with a nave 90ft long by 24ft wide, and, unusually, side aisles of similar dimensions. The impression was of light and space with windows in the nave vault and around every wall. There was a brass commemorating Thomas, 10th Lord Berkeley (of Berkeley Castle) and Margaret his wife. He was 14, she seven when they married. 'In youth our parents joined our hands, ourselves our hearts. This tombe our bodyes hath, the heavens our better parts.' She died aged 31, he never remarried. He was Admiral of the King's Fleet and fought at Agincourt in 1415, dying on 13th July 1417, aged 64.

Out of Wotton I climbed Wotton Hill to an enclosed area containing nine tall but straggly fir trees, known as the Jubilee Plantation, originally planted in 1815 to celebrate the victory at Waterloo. From one of the many seats I enjoyed magnificent views of Wotton and to the Severn (the bridge again). There was a pleasant, cooling breeze. This was some of the best walking terrain—a path in woods, cool, shaded, level, soft, and firm. In mid-afternoon I came to the impressive William Tyndale memorial, erected in 1866. A plaque informed me that he was: 'Translator of the English bible who first caused the New Testament to be printed in the mother tongue of his countrymen. Born near this spot (near North Nibley) he suffered martyrdom at Vilvorde, Flanders in 1536.'

Later I was lost again, this time in the woods at the top of Stinchcombe Hill, until I saw white spots denoting the Cotswold Way high up on trees, three or four of them. Ingenious. Coming down from the woods I met a man tending two horses. He said there was nowhere to stay in Dursley, my intended destination, and if I liked I could camp in one of his fields. As we chatted he told me a story of a lord or earl from near St Austell in Somerset who couldn't face up to things when his home, a castle, was in financial trouble. He walked out one day and went on the road. Some time later he met a gypsy or traveller who jumped down from his cart and pressed some money into his hand. The lord thought there was still some humanity left in the world, went home and restored his fortunes. The man, who was short, stocky with gingerish moustache and goatee beard, said I might see deer and buzzard. "We give the buzzards first choice of the young rabbits, then get rid of a few ourselves. They're a nuisance, as well as the foxes. Saw one the other day dying of poison—strychnine—not very pleasant." He explained that the lane I was on ran from Berkeley Castle to Cirencester, and had been used in Roman days and before. He rolled a cigarette and drove off on a tractor up the field.

After pitching the tent I went into town past Canadian style wood houses (after the 'wreckers'—locals who emigrated to Canada and then came back). Behind the bar in the Yew Tree was a beautiful girl called Ann, with black hair, classic features, and lovely mouth and teeth. She had bare arms and spoke with a Gloucestershire accent, though her mother was from Cyprus and now lived in Rhodes, from where she sent her olive oil which she loved.

### *Wednesday, 16th July*

Woke at 3.30 a.m. to the cracking of a gate being forced open and horses coming into my field. I couldn't fall asleep again, being fearful of the horses coming too close to the tent, indeed one nudged the back where my head was, another the front. I got up hurriedly and they moved off, whereupon nature called and I used the trowel again. I decided to evict the horses from the field and spent nearly an hour in rounding them up and closing the gate once more. It made for an early start.

There was also an unbelievable start to the walking day. I got onto the golf course and back on my route, only to find signs taking me into woods and literally down to where I started from yesterday. So once more it was a case of retracing my steps, crossing the course and asking those by the clubhouse. "Had a good game?" I asked the one who knew where the path went.

"Not really, I was playing on my own," said the elderly gentleman. Another member didn't know the path was there in all the years he had been a member, and had never noticed the waymarking signs.

By 10 a.m. I had gained Dursley where I visited the Gents, usefully equipped with soap, water and hot air, and then a tea-room. Physically refreshed I now sought the spiritual variety and went into

34

Dursley Church where there is a wooden carving of Mary and Child by Charles Albert Preater, 1896-1974, called 'Fruit of the mystic Rose'. The church is light and spacious and there is a lovely stained glass window at the east end of the nave depicting the Ascension. I took some time to meditate. From the village I walked up Cam Peak with beautiful views all round.

Having passed a couple, probably Dutch, coming the other way, I reached the top of Cam Long Down where I passed a boy with three full black plastic bags. "I've been pulling out ragwort since nine and it doesn't show much. I'm going to lunch now." I thought that was a good idea and had my own, a Cornish pasty, and was joined by a middle-aged couple. The man was chatty, telling me there were plans to build even more houses and that Dursley and Cam would soon be joined together. He pointed out the Malvern Hills in the distance and the Sugar Loaf near Abergavenny. "People have gone to other parts of the world and come back and said they've seen nothing like this view."

As I pressed on during the afternoon, the right side of my body began hurting—my foot, shoulder, even behind my ear. When I reached Frocester Hill at Coaley Peak, I realised I had only walked five miles in the day. But did it really matter? For I had observed lots of butterflies and swallows and had had the benefit of wonderful views. At the summit's picnic tables I was joined by several dogs and a family group. An elderly lady with white hair from London said: "It's like Bangladesh. I'm glad we got away." Two of the four dogs, all different makes, were from the RSPCA. The family drank lemonade and ate crisps, offering me some too. A woman, brown, soft spoken and friendly, said: "We seem to be disturbing your peace and quiet."

Despite feeling tired, and aching, I pressed on through King's Stanley and past Nympsfield long barrow. Soon after 6 p.m. I reached the outskirts of Stonehouse, an area full of wrecked cars and an electricity generating station—not a very auspicious entrance to a town. I entered the town, passing Wycliffe School, with its artificial surface playing field. Funny, when you are specifically looking for something, it doesn't appear. There was no sign of a B & B anywhere, but over a pint of Brains bitter in the Globe Inn I found out where the nearest were and soon came to Merton House on leaving the village, a delightful B & B.

### Thursday, 17th July

At breakfast I sat with a Mr Lloyd, a burly ex-Marine, staying on business. He worked for a local company that had something to do with radio and environmental control. We talked about mobiles. I said I had planned to buy one specially for this walk, but decided against it because I wouldn't be able to use it a lot of the time due to where I'd be. "They don't yet cover vast areas of the country, only population areas," he said, adding "Some lads are buying cheap mobiles which ring and then hold pretend conversations." He had travelled the world as a Royal Marine and on snow exercises in Norway had to carry a 60lb pack. Mrs. Hodge, the landlady, said I looked very slim. I said my trousers were nearly falling down I had lost so much weight and she produced an old fashioned, 50 year-old instrument for making holes in leather. I made another hole in my belt. "Every service provided," she smiled. At 10 a.m. I left, and soon became lost. A young lad with a squashed nose helped me locate Westrup. "Where you from?"

"Land's End."

"Where's that?"

"Cornwall."

"Gee. Where you going?"

"John O'Groats —in Scotland."

"You walking all the way to Scotland?"

During the day I passed three fit young men doing remedial work in the woods, laying wooden beams along the track for the National Trust. They said they didn't know the End to End route came through the Cotswold Way!

At a car park further along I passed a hearty couple finishing their walk and going to their car. The man asked whether I was doing the Cotswold Way. "And some," I replied, "Land's End to John O'Groats."

"Is it some kind of penance?" asked the woman from a tanned face.

"You might be right," I said.

Yet further along I came to Cliff Well, a small building housing a stopped well, but still with an old handle. A plaque read: 'Deo Gratius - Whoever the Bucketful upwindeth, Let him bless God, who water findeth: Yet water here but small availeth, Go seek that well which never faileth. John C4, V14.' After seeing a deer—a glimpse of a red-haired animal—I was about to hug a beech tree, only to find it was covered in slugs. I asked myself whether I felt enlightened at all. I certainly felt more aware, more aware of nature, but I hadn't got on very well with people. It was nice to speak to the animals as you went along.

By 4 p.m. I arrived in Painswick and was confronted by a choice of B & Bs. The one I chose was run by an elderly couple, and I was promptly told: "Take your boots off." The woman told me that the post office was the oldest in the country and they were bringing out a special stamp of it. I was soon in the tea shop enjoying tea and cream cake before investigating this old post office; the lady behind the counter said the building was Victorian and confirmed that in August a commemorative stamp was coming out. It was also going to feature on TV and they would all have to dress up. Another lady in the gifts section said it was 13th century. She was, however, suspicious about the shoes in a glass case that were supposed to be a couple of hundred years old and had been found above a baker's oven and used to keep witches away—one shoe looked as if it had metal lace holes. She vowed to check the history of shoes. Outside a sign said the building was in fact 15th century—but it was still the oldest post office in the country. I was told that the next door cottage was also very old and was where the hangman used to stay. The story went that one hangman was called out one day only to find it was for his son, caught scrumping apples. His was just one of 36 ghosts who appeared in the village.

I walked through the churchyard which was full of well clipped yew trees, to see the stocks, then talked to a tall old gentleman. He told me another Painswick story with confusing numbers. Apparently there were only ever 99 yew trees, because every time a new one took root, another would die. However, someone counted them recently and there were 103. He liked living in Painswick, having lived in the country where it was a seven mile journey to get a loaf of bread. He was appalled at the idea of Stroud Council wanting to build 1,400 houses in Painswick Valley—I had seen many protest posters in windows. Surely they could go somewhere else, he felt, and not spoil the beauty of the area, which, anyway, was a conservation area. He added that there was always something going on in the village and lots of Japanese and American tourists visited.

Back at the B & B I took remedial action on my feet, especially the right one, of which the small toe was very swollen and pus was coming out. In the evening I used the Royal Oak for sustenance, both liquid and solid. They did an excellent pint of Flowers. I seemed to be splashing out. Was I celebrating? I supposed I was half-way along the Cotswold Way.

*Friday, 18th July*

I felt good after an excellent meditation. Although time consuming, these sessions allowed me to keep my equilibrium, both in body and mind. Breakfast was an international affair, involving a middle-aged Norwegian couple, an Austrian and an American woman. The Norwegians, the woman was a lawyer, loved coming to Britain for walking holidays. They had been to the Lake District, Scotland, Yorkshire Dales and were now walking north to south along the Cotswold Way. They hadn't met any other walkers. They approved of the British system of footpaths, saying that in Norway farmers wouldn't let you walk through fields of corn, as they had done here. They talked about the European Union and why Norway hadn't joined—the husband wanted Norway to join, the woman didn't, so, like religion, they don't usually talk about it—as well as about adoption and drugs in Norway. This brought in the American who was something to do with child adoption in California, whilst the Austrian thought it better to keep the drug problem open.

After another stroll around the village, I eventually left mid-morning, heading across the golf course to Painswick Beacon. This gave me a lovely view of a town and a huge industrial area. As I was not quite sure where I was, when a party of schoolchildren appeared

I asked their teacher. He identified the outskirts of Gloucester, the cathedral, Duponts, and to the right Cheltenham and the Government Communications Headquarters. In front, fenced off to prevent erosion, was Cooper's Hill down which they roll the 7lb Gloucester cheeses. It looked very steep. "People get drunk and get killed," the teacher said, "and three years ago some were struck by lightning and killed. It's a fertility rite." At the bottom of the hill I visited the Haven tea garden, recommended by the teacher. The owner, Rosemary Hellerman, said she was resting after the children's visit. She said there were not so many walkers these days on the Cotswold Way, and she let me look through her folder of leaflets and newspaper cuttings on the cheese rolling. In the old days, she said, everybody used to dress up in their Sunday best including her father. I sat in a hammock having tea and scones in the warm sunshine while leafing through the pages. I read that it was a 3 in 1 hill and that there were usually between six and 12 runners taking part, the first one down the hill winning. There were different classes. Eight people were indeed hurt by lightning in 1982—spectators who were standing under a tree.

"They must be crackers" a heading stated. Another report read: "Cheese Rolling Wake - Gods of paganism and superstition through to the Christian calendar and the one True God. Easter worship of the sun - Whitsun May Day." It was good training, all the spills, for the St John Ambulance Brigade. I sat back and enjoyed the lovely view of fruit trees and the hills beyond. Butterflies were fluttering around; a big one, russet red colour with four eyes, flexed its wings on the table top in the sun. There was a smell of mint and I felt drowsy. It was very peaceful—only a faint hum from the motorway and the drone of an aircraft. Perfect! Almost a mystical feeling. I was nodding off when I was woken by a ginger cat jumping on my lap. I realised it was 4 p.m. and reluctantly had to leave. As I couldn't make Mrs Hellerman hear, I left quietly leaving my money on the tray. Further on I passed a strange looking pea crop—rape gone to seed. The pod contained seeds (like pepper) from which comes the oil used in unnamed vegetable oils and margarine. The lovely blue flowered crop I had also seen was flax, the seeds from which yield linseed oil.

The early evening was spent at the Air Balloon, a prominent pub at a busy junction near Birdlip. A notice informed me that many balloon ascents were made from this spot from 1784 onwards, including one by Walter Powell, who ascended from Malmesbury and disappeared without trace. That evening I pitched the tent in a wood off the track. My feet appeared to be improving and I had covered 10 miles today in eight hours.

### Saturday, 19th July

A rotten night, couldn't get warm. At one point some children went past flashing torches. "Look, someone's camping over there," flash, flash. "Wouldn't like to camp there."

Whilst performing nature's morning call, a worm type thing broke earth, looked around startled and disappeared, fearful of being drowned or worse. Once underway it felt good to be out in the sun and out of the cold of the wood. Leckhampton Hill provided a good view over Cheltenham, and I could understand why the topograph on the summit had been sponsored by the Nixon family in memory of Roger of that ilk who enjoyed living and walking on the hill for 40 years. All along the ridge I followed a family, but we never spoke. Funny, really. Coming off the hill I stopped for a party of 60 walkers, of all ages, and asked a woman who they were but she was too puffed to reply.

The route passed through Lineover Woods to the Reservoir Inn, a life-saver as it was still open for a couple of pints of Boddingtons, though not food. 'Everywhere you go always take the weather' was on the radio, rather a nice sentiment. Further on there was a B & B which sold chocolate, on which I stocked up. I was apparently their third End to Ender that year, one going the other way three weeks ago.

Dowdeswell Wood was full of butterflies and dragonflies and there were plenty of informative boards about the different trees. The only distraction was the crackling coming from overhead power cables. Further on, however, two people were out with shotguns, yet further on was a motorbike playground, where two bikers were doing their thing, with plenty of revving up and noise, whilst overhead two strange looking aircraft passed. I wondered whether there was an air show on.

As the afternoon ended I entered the Bill Smyllie reserve (named after the man whose generous donation enabled the purchase of the land), and feeling whacked, chose a spot to camp that had a lovely view though along with dung heaps, thistles and flies. As I ate my meal I heard someone going past say: "There's someone camping behind the hedge. It shouldn't be allowed." And again coming back, walking a dog, someone said "I don't think it's legal."

*Sunday, 20th July*

Today was a day of surprises. The first was to find that Cleeve golf club had a restaurant open to the public. Arriving just after 10 a.m. I ordered brunch. It also allowed me to top up my water bottle, which I also did later from the first stream I'd seen for a while—would I survive!

The path passed Belas Knap long barrow which contains the remains of 38 human skeletons plus animal bones, flint implements and pottery, all dating from around 3000 B.C. It seemed to be a walkers' mecca, with one party having lunch, a party of American walkers arriving followed by four half-naked walkers as I left.

In the early afternoon I arrived in Winchcombe and visited St Peter's Church, which dominates the village. Winchcombe's importance as one of the main towns in the kingdom of Mercia centred on the Benedictine Abbey that stood next to the church, with its shrine to King Kenelm being a place of pilgrimage into the Middle Ages. There is a lovely wooden vault over the nave, but I most admired a wooden box with iron fittings. A sign stated: 'Alms box, 1547 - an injunction of Edward VI decreed that there should be three locks making the opening possible only in presence of the vicar and both church wardens.' Underneath was added a note: 'Vandalised, please do not use.' A wall plaque read: 'Sacred to the memory of Mary wife of William Best daughter of John and Ann Timbrell who died Aug 13 1826. Aged 61 years. She was - but words are wanting to express What She Was, think what a good wife ought to be: and she was that.' Back outside, I looked at the gargoyles, a popular feature of the church. In the 1620s to 1670 I learnt that tobacco was grown in the locality in defiance of authority.

I then made a surprise call on my cousin, Brenda, though was sidetracked *en route* into having a cream tea. This was followed by further tea with Brenda. She is amazing—she just doesn't stop talking and is like a machine gun spitting out words. During our conversation she told me about her love for Jaramie, her late husband. She didn't want a counsellor when he died. "I sent him away. I couldn't speak to a complete stranger." But neither could she cry until she was in Boots in Cheltenham one day and saw a hair-dryer called Babe. "Jaramie always called me Babe because of my small hands," she went on. "I couldn't stop crying, tears fell from my face, even out in the road." Jaramie had twice escaped from Czechoslovakia—the first time as an escaping resistance fighter during the Second World War, and then again after the war fleeing, with Brenda, from the communists. They had been in the bungalow only a year before he died—he had had gangrene and initially lost a leg. "Ours was a true love. Other people can't understand what it was like."

Before leaving Winchcombe I visited the 15th century coaching inn, the White Lion, for a pint of Timothy Taylor Landlord, another of Caledonian 80 shilling and then a Marston's Pedigree. Think I preferred the Landlord. "Are you from CAMRA?" asked the barman, a large man with a beer stomach and ginger hair, once he saw my notebook. I left through wheatfields, freeing a red butterfly from a spider's web, wondering if I was doing the right thing, and headed for Hailes. A music festival was being held in the 12th century church, built before the abbey and which has been recently restored. Two elderly people were in the graveyard resting against tombstones as they listened to what a notice told me was Schubert's 'Cradle Song'. It was lovely. I walked past the entrance to the ruins of Hailes Abbey and, *en route* to Beckbury Camp, I pitched my tent in an open field with sheep.

### Monday, 21st July

A disturbed night, thanks to the wind flapping the tent and a nearby bird scarer banging away all night. The day was overcast and so muggy, making me short and irritable with those I met. Nevertheless, it was a change to walk past cabbages as opposed to wheat and corn. A group of rams in another field looked uncomfortable with their dangling ball sacks. I soon came to Stanway, but Monday was not a good day to visit this area. The tea-rooms were closed, as were Stanway House and parish church. Nevertheless, the cricket pitch had an unusual but most attractive pavilion with a verandah under a broad sweeping thatched roof and raised above the ground on mushroom-looking staddle stones.

The church in the next village, Stanton, was just my type. It's very small, with just 21 small wooden pews, and upstairs at the back of the nave are more seats underneath the organ, itself close to the plain wooden timber roof. In the village are short rows of cottages built of local stone, now beautifully mellow, and equally warm coloured tile roofs with dormer windows. Creepers and flowers added to the affect. I stopped at the village inn for refreshment by Donnington best bitter.

During the afternoon, as I climbed out of a field of sheep, my mood improved and I spoke to a lady walking two Collie dogs, one of which was cooling itself in a stream. She liked walking but suffered arthritis in the knee (caused by wearing Wellington boots over a long time). Her husband, aged 80, also walked a lot but now found he too was getting arthritis in the knee. "It's a question of wear and tear when you reach our age," she said. But she thought the best way to keep fit was walking. She hoped Broadway would soon get its bypass—too much traffic.

I found Broadway touristy and expensive—certainly for tea and cake, and was happy to head out of the town and aim for Broadway Tower, a folly built for the 6th Earl of Coventry. The Pre-Raphaelite painters Morris, Rossetti and Burne-Jones used to visit. As I continued I saw a herd of red deer wandering in the grounds, and further on found a topograph which showed: Worcester 23m, John O'Groats 613m, Edinburgh 323m, Land's End 253m, Chipping

Camden 3m. Still a fair way to go! In the early evening I approached Dover's Hill which, I learnt from a plaque, takes its name from a colourful local barrister called Robert Dover, the hillside having been the venue for his Cotswold Olimpick Games which he began in 1612. Apparently Dover used to be MC of the games, mounted on a white horse, and events were started by a cannon fired from an imitation castle. These were celebrated until 1852 when they were stopped by the enclosure of Dover's Hill as part of the parish of Weston Subedge. They were revived in 1951 as a one-off for the Festival of Britain, when the games included horse racing and coursing; field events of jumping, leaping, and throwing a sledge-hammer; spurning and pitching the bar; and combative games of quarter staff fencing, wrestling, and shin-kicking. From 1963 they were revived on an annual basis, the area now being owned by the National Trust. Amazing to think I'd never heard about these Games before. Finally I entered Chipping Campden and finished the Cotswold Way walk at the church of St James. I celebrated with a pint of Hambleton's Thoroughbred, one of six cask ales in the Volunteer Arms.

Unfortunately the pub's accommodation was full, as were all the B & Bs. I finally tried the Red Lion hotel, where an attractive blonde barmaid greeted me with "Hello traveller." The landlady explained she had a single left as part of a family suite of two rooms, and though it was expensive I decided to take it. I went to bed worrying about finances—had I enough to continue!

# 4. Heart of England & Staffordshire Ways

*Tuesday, 22nd July*

Not a good night's sleep, for it was too hot and stuffy. Breakfast was reached by stepping over a boxer dog outside my room that was playing with a bone. By 9.15 a.m. the cleaning woman wanted to come into my room. I phoned my bank and discovered I still had £748 in my account, more than I had thought, so I decided to carry on. It would be nice to have a break, with Great Malvern and Jenny's home not that far away, but it could be harmful to the system! So, having bought a book on the Heart of England Way, I took to the local tea-room to work out the next stages of the route. This was followed by a visit to St James' church, which was rebuilt during the 15th century when Campden was a prosperous centre of the wool trade.

Then it was off to start the Heart of England Way. This was very much new territory for me and I hadn't heard of any of the places I was going to. I soon appreciated I might not yet see them, for I was quickly lost once more, refound my way, then lost it again. Retracing my steps into Mickleton I read several plaques: 'Bledisloe Cup - best kept village competition - winners 1995'; 'Gloucestershire branch Runners-up 1991'; 'Highly Commended 1989'. They seemed as confused as I was. Eventually I took to the B road which somewhat

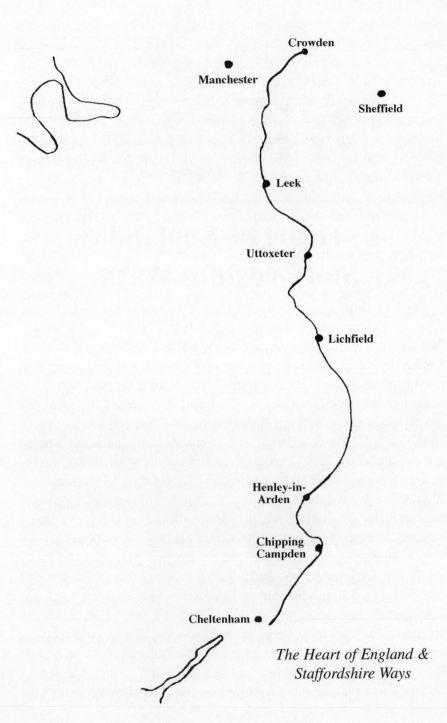

*The Heart of England &
Staffordshire Ways*

shadowed the long distance path. From Upper Quinton I retook to the path and at some point crossed into Warwickshire. I was soon walking in a field alongside security fencing protecting debris, huts and caravans. In another field and through a hedge I could see stand seats and lights through a wall of sorts, very high. Eventually I reached Long Marston and the Marston Arms where I had a pint of Boddington Manchester Gold. It was creamy, but cold, too cold for me. So I next had a pint of ordinary Boddingtons. Soon after leaving the pub I decided to pitch the tent in a big open field with sheep. I had not long settled in when a 4-wheel drive pick-up, with lots of lights, approached. A man with a black beard looked at me. "Do you mind if I camp here?" I asked instantly.

"Are you on the footpath?"

"Yes."

"Well, have a good time." Later, I was woken by raucous laughter and triumphant cries from a nearby pub.

### Wednesday, 23rd July

After a fitful sleep, it was time to reorientate myself. By the time I had, I'd confused the local cows. I soon arrived in Dorsington, a village of thatched cottages, and a green by the church of St Peter. Its door was open, its key being in the lock, and inside I found Jean. She said the church was usually locked because of theft, thieves now even stealing pulpits. She was a true local, her great grandparents being married in the church in the 1850s, twenty years before it was renovated. She also enlightened me on my puzzle of the previous day—the disused airfield I had passed was now used for the Phoenix Pop Festival. It was apparently like a county show without the animals, and she had helped run a Scouts stall. She had been amazed at all the different hair styles, colours and ornaments; but thought they all seemed nice people. She was also something to do with the Heart of England Way, helping put up signs and styles and asked me if the paths were all right. I mentioned that the Heart of England Way was much quieter than the Cotswold Way—I had hardly seen another walker.

Shortly after leaving the village I saw a traveller lying on the edge of a field, but he looked away. I passed through Barton, got lost, came back and went into the pub—where else—and puzzled over maps over some Theakston's best bitter. I left as the pub filled up and came to a field of onions where a gang of Indian looking pickers were taking a break. I chatted to one of them with grey bristles, Wellington boots and clutching a Carlsberg Special Brew can and carrier bag who was resting by a style. He moaned about the work. "No union. We work until 2 or 3 o'clock. When we finish with the onions it's leeks. Then in one week's time no work. Have to mortgage house. Last year very good. This year no good. Everywhere."

Through Bidford-on-Avon, with its nice bridge over the river, a meadow with people playing, its pubs, cafés and shops, but locked church. I became temporarily lost again. Eventually I reached Broom along roads, as the footpath petered out, and thence Wixford, and another closed church.

In the early evening I arrived in Alcester, a pleasant looking town, with a lovely row of old barns, probably almshouses. Passing an old lady who was sitting on a park bench, I said hello, and she asked me whether I was going home (wish I was!). "I like sitting here," she said. "Can't bear being in my flat all the time. I used to live in a bungalow with a small front and back garden, but my daughter wanted me to move here. I haven't the heart to tell her, but I've lived here for 12 months and I don't like it. I've joined the local Baptist church and learnt to play whist. But it's only to get out. I shouldn't be talking to you." I didn't know what to say, so I just said goodbye and continued on. I soon fell into the Royal Oak for a pint of Smith's cask bitter, but the pub was too commercialised. The 'Karaoke at the Oake' sign summed it up.

Leaving the town I found a suitable field and decided to camp near the trail. Whilst cooking supper—soup and cooked apricots and dates, for a change—I watched a hot air balloon, purple with ice-lolly type patches, in the valley below. I could see its flame from time to time as it journeyed northwards and eventually out of sight. It was lovely to simply look at the sky—and ignore how smelly I felt.

*Thursday, 24th July*

Woke at 8 a.m., as overnight rain stopped. The weather was cooler, thank heavens. Approaching a pond at the corner of a field, a heron flew up and made its ungainly exit. Further on I walked across a field of ploughed up peas, and harvested some of those that had been missed. Later I added some equally delicious broad beans, before coming across another heron, a stone statue by a dried-up pond.

In the early afternoon I reached Henley-in-Arden with its one mile long High Street containing seven pubs, two hotels and five restaurants. I selected Henley's ice-cream parlour, where I had cream tea and Henley's strawberry ice cream. I sat at the same table as a young man in brown, with a growth of beard and wearing a BBC Pebble Mill baseball cap. "Walking?" he asked. "Feel knackered, do you? Got lots of money?"

"Just enough," I replied. I took my notebook out.

"Ah, writing are you, writing a book?" When my tea arrived he said: "You must be a millionaire," before gulping down a cup from the pot of tea he had ordered, suddenly getting up saying "All the best mate" and leaving. I saw him get into a taxi which had been waiting.

One of the parlour maids told me the ice cream was made in a factory at the back of the shop, but unfortunately the council was closing it down following complaints of noise by neighbours, and it was moving to Stourbridge. "It will be Henley's loss," I said.

"Yes, there are over 100 people working here and at lunchtime they go to the local shops, cafés and pubs."

I then called into the Heritage Centre next door where I had a cup of tea in the newly opened café. The centre included a school-room, arranged as it would have been in Victorian times. I was told by the man changing the price list that the centre owed its existence to a mega-rich American, now in his 80s, who had made his money in the leisure trade. He had bought the Lord of the Manor title and this building which dated back to the 13th century. A plaque read: 'Heritage Centre made possible by generosity of former Lord of the Manor, Joseph Hardy, of Pittsburgh, and inaugurated by his daughter Robin Hardy Freed, the present head, in November 1996.' Joseph

Hardy is now building a replica of the Ritz Hotel in Pennsylvania. I decided to stay on in Henley at a B & B recommended by the centre, and *en route* I visited the 15th century church of St John the Baptist. This has lovely designs in its stained glass windows. I continued up the wide main street, tree-lined and flower-bedecked, with a number of interesting timber-framed buildings. Flowers also surrounded the 15th century market cross, or rather its shaft, and I recalled that the woman in the Heritage Centre tea room had said "You are seeing Henley at its best because of the Bloom competition."

The B & B proved to be a Georgian house standing in 220 acres of land. Originally Lapworth Hall, the farm was renamed Ireland's after Robert Ireland who farmed there in 1500. The owner, Pam, agreed to do some laundry for me while I had a nice hot bath. Then I visited the Bird in Hand, recommended by Pam. The beer was Strongarm, a ruby red bitter from Camerons, a Hartlepool brewery, and the landlord got the barmaid to first pour some out to show me its colour and taste. The associated meal was excellent and enormous, so I decided to buy the chef, waiter and kitchen helper a drink.

On the TV news I learnt that the government intends to do something about battery chickens, but wants it banned by the EU which will take time. They should ban it straight away, it's so cruel.

### Friday, 25th July

It felt good to be up—refreshed, clean and everything washed. My spirits were high. Pam advised me of a short cut to rejoin the Heart of England Way, instead of travelling three miles into Henley and out again. For once I managed to follow directions that had been given to me, and I was soon in Lowsonford, where I rested by the Stratford-upon-Avon Canal and watched a narrow boat going through a lock. I spotted a large mushroom on the verge and picked it. Soon after I crossed the noisy M40 into the second wind-flattened wheat field of the day. The church of St Laurence in Rowington was shut, but I rested on a bench in the graveyard.

The church at Baddesley Clinton was open, however, a notice stating 'St Michael's church is now open following the installation of a 24 hour surveillance system.' Inside another read: 'Beneath this

*The author at the start of the walk, his shadow,*
*and trying out the tent before setting off*

*Glastonbury Tor (top left), Wotton-under-Edge parish church (top right),
New thatch in Devonshire (below)*

*Tea garden, Cooper's Hill (top left), Cheese rolling site at
Cooper's Hill (top right), Overlooking Bath (below)*

*Stanton village (top), Market Cross and Cross House,*
*Henley-in-Arden (lower left), Berkswell Church porch (lower right)*

*Lichfield Cathedral*

*The sleeping children in Lichfield Cathedral (top),
Memorial to Cdr Edward Smith of the Titanic in Lichfield (lower left) The
Essex bridge—the longest packhorse bridge in England—
at Shugborough Hall (lower right)*

*Caldon Canal, nr. Cheddleton (top)*
*The author at the farmhouse ruins at Top Withens (below)*

*Which way? Even in Japanese near Haworth!*

*Accommodation and refreshments: Bothy near Traquair (top left),
Yearning Saddle shelter (top right), Sheep cratch snack bar seen* en route
*(centre), Tea-room at Horneystead farm (lower)*

*Assorted animals seen* en route*:*
*Ostriches near Zeal Monachorum (top), Reindeer antlers in Abbots*
*Bromley (centre left), Tethered pig near St Erth (centre right),*
*Llamas at Berriedale Braes (lower)*

*Waterfalls: High Force (top left), Low Force (centre left),*
*Falls of Tarf (top right),*
*Cauldron Snout (lower)*

*Opposite page: Gargoyle on St Peter's Church, Winchcombe (top left),*
*Drinking fountain, Middleton-in-Teesdale (top right),*
*JCB man nr. Denstone (centre left), Sculpture in Hathersleigh*
*market (lower left), White Nancy folly (bottom right)*
*This page: Black Watch memorial, Aberfeldy (top left), Flodden statue,*
*Selkirk (top right), Mungo Park monument, Selkirk (lower)*

*Haworth graveyard, containing the graves of 40,000 villagers (top),*
*Double bridge across the Leeds & Liverpool Canal*
*to carry the A59 (centre), Bowes Castle keep (lower)*

*River Teesdale (top), Goldsborough gritstone outcrop (centre), Sheep at deserted Halsted Farm near Dufton (lower)*

*Looking across the Lake District from Cross Fell (top), On top of Great Dun Fell (centre), Whinstone Cliffs, Hadrian's Wall (lower)*

*Camped by Hadrian's Wall (top),*
*Forestry activity in Wark Forest (centre), Byrness Church (lower)*

*Kelso Abbey*

*Cheviot Hills from near Russell's Cairn (top),*
*View northwards from near the Schil (lower)*

*Opposite page:*
*Melrose Abbey (top), Abbotsford House (centre),*
*Neidpath Castle, Peebles (lower)*
*This page:*
*The church and Bridge Inn, Peebles (top),*
*Looking back to Aberfeldy (lower)*

*River Tilt near Blair Atholl (top),*
*Glen Tilt (lower)*

*Bynack Burn (top), Lairig Ghru, with Devil's Point on the left, and Ben Macdui on the right (centre), Loch Fleet, north of Dornoch (lower)*

*Journey's end*

chapel repose 12 generations of the Ferrers of Baddesley Clinton from Sir Edward who died in 1535.' There was a side tomb to Sir Edward Ferrers and on the wall memorials to two more members of the family. Ferrers are also depicted in the beautiful east window. Further on I passed the mediaeval Manor House, owned by the Ferrers for 500 years, but now owned and run by the National Trust. For once I thought it best not to dally and carried on to Chadwick End where I couldn't resist popping in to the Orange Tree. For once the beer, Flowers best bitter, was cloudy. I almost missed the Heart of England Way on leaving the village, and then found a 'No Cycling' sign in the middle of fields of grass and broad beans. I was feeling good and progress was likewise, further stimulated by finding another pub, this one keeping Burton Ale.

Once again I lost my way, but a passing cyclist put me right. As I approached Berkswell I saw a suitable piece of grass and, although very close to the village, I pitched the tent. Supper consisted of home made vegetable stew from produce harvested along the way: fresh peas, beans and mushroom, complemented with rice, dahl and ginger. However, I paid the penalty for my temerity in camping close to the church—bell practice started and went on and on and on. Although the peel of church bells on a Sunday is fine, when they are just practising - ugh!

### Saturday, 26th July

Rotten night. Very cold. As well as my anorak I had to put on over-trousers as the foil blanket had torn and has had it. I would have to consider getting a lightweight sleeping bag. To add to the cold, there was also the noise—three times aircraft went directly overhead, whilst the church bells chimed every hour. That church, the very splendid 12th century church of St John Baptist, was well worth the visit. In the chancel were beautifully carved modern (1909) stalls. Upstairs there was a room used for small services and meetings, and below was a crypt with a large wooden cross. My meditation was disturbed by rats scuffling in the loft and by two people entering the church. The 16th century porch had a priest's room above, which was later used as the village school, parish council house and now as the vestry.

I stocked up on provisions at the village store and the owner asked me where I came from and where I was going to. "Thought you were slim. Whew. Any violence? Nobody tried to attack you?" Turning to a woman he added "Do you hear that, all the way from Land's End." Two builders erecting scaffolding on the building opposite asked whether I was camping, and then wanted to join me.

On the outskirts of the village I met my young cyclist friend from yesterday. He told me of a programme on TV about farmers throwing walkers off their land, in Hereford, Wales and Scotland. Changing tack he reckoned that in 10 years time Berkswell would be built up, there was already a housing estate at Balsall Common.

In a wheat field I saw a sign: 'Beware! Jet spray may fire at any time'. At least that was preferable to the sign seen the day before: 'Dangerous chemicals sprayed'. In Meriden stood the locked parish church of St Laurence, founded in a forest by a missionary sent out by Lady Godiva nearly 1,000 years earlier. A quarter of a mile away, on the village green, was a 500 year-old cross with the sign: 'This ancient wayside cross has stood in the village for some 500 years and by tradition it marks the CENTRE OF ENGLAND. The cross was rebuilt on this site when the Green was improved in celebration of the Festival of Britain, 1951.' There were also memorial plaques to cyclists. At the Spar shop I bought more supplies and a turbanned gentleman at the till gave me a bar of chocolate as I left, a lovely gesture. Just beyond Meriden I spotted another worrying sign: 'Forest Enterprise Warning - chemical spraying. Forestry Commission.' Signposts tell me that Coventry is only 5 miles from Meriden and Solihull 7 miles from Berkswell, yet it is amazing how rural the route is, though now it lies largely through fields of oil seed rape. I began to wonder if farmers actually harvest the stuff or let it rot, it was so knocked about. Further on I saw a sign saying: 'Welcome to Solihull'. Passing through more fields of rape which tripped me up and smelt of bad cabbages, I began to feel as if I was drowning in the wretched stuff. Finally I found a good spot to set up camp.

## Sunday, 27th July

Had an unsettled night, and made a late start, making the excuse to myself that it was Sunday. It also meant that there were more walkers about and people to chat to. The first was a man with a stick and a dog who asked "Have you seen anyone shooting? My dog's picked up two injured pigeons. I want to find out who it is." I hadn't heard a shot. In Shustoke I passed a middle-aged woman who remarked "I try to walk to the reservoir every day, or at least go by bike. I've lived here all my life, but it's only just a short time ago they've opened the paths. I'm making the most of it."

Having lunch just past a reservoir, whilst sitting on a grassy patch by the railway line, a middle-aged couple stopped for a chat, which turned to what there was to see in Lichfield, my next major centre of population. Both were in shorts and carried haversacks, and were doing the Heart of England Way in stages. They'd walked the Cotswold Way one and a half years previously.

The afternoon involved more rape, and, for variety, a military firing range. Thence on through Hurley to Kingsbury, and a pint of Bass. I then trekked on to the Broomey Croft campsite which had been recommended by the couple out walking. At the camp shop I bought ice-cream, milk and Twix. Having pitched the tent, and with the sun still very hot, I consumed the lot. The nearby waterpark, opened in 1975, is based on 600 acres of disused gravel workings and has wildlife and outdoor pursuits.

## Monday, 28th July

The noise from the nearby motorway reverberated all night, and in the morning I was disturbed by the sound of the site's lawnmower. As I packed up, the warden said "It's wonderful. I do admire you for what you are doing. Fulfilling your dreams." Today's route led along the Birmingham and Fazeley Canal, and it was a pleasant saunter, with no worries about wrong turnings. At times I watched martins or swallows dive-bombing the water, just touching it with their belly. The canal water initially looked murky, but later on it cleared and it was then I came across several fishermen. One had two boxes of large wriggling maggots, one collection light brown, the other a pinky red. "Surprising how the fish seem to have a preference for colour," he said. "These others," pointing to dead maggots, going dark brown, "are casters. If you don't put them in the fridge, they would become flies. Fish like these too."—but he had only caught one fish all morning. Further on I came to a bizarre footbridge over the canal with twin white turrets over which I climbed.

At Drayton Bassett I bought supplies from the shop. "Can I sit outside?" I asked the lady, pointing to two seats in the front garden.

"Park your bum and make yourself comfortable," she said. "That's what they're there for." Next door was St Peter's Church, but it was locked. There was much rubbish near the door, itself close to the ugly grave of Sir Robert Peel (5th Baronet) who died on 6th April 1934, aged 35 years. He was the descendant of *the* Sir Robert Peel, former Prime Minister and founder of the police force, who lived in Drayton Manor which is now run as a zoo.

In the afternoon I came across the first ripe blackberries on the trip—they tasted delicious and I had quite a feast, and as the evening came on I couldn't believe my luck when I saw another Caravanning and Camping sign. However, the site turned out to be derelict—an old 'Fresh Cream today' sign hung in the closed office/shop. The nearby toilets were boarded up and there were still two caravans, probably derelict, and a field of raspberry canes had gone to waste, the berries black and dry. Although it looked a bit forlorn there was a nice patch of grass, so I decided to stay.

*Tuesday, 29th July*

Today was just going to be a short walk into Lichfield, a city I wanted to explore, as well as acquiring guidebooks for the next stages. On the outskirts of the city a man who was busily cutting his lawn, stopped and ran down to me and asked if I was doing the Heart of England Way. When I told him what I was doing he exclaimed "You're a hero" and invited me in for a cup of tea and a biscuit. Gerald, retired and a keen walker, introduced me to his wife, Jean, telling me of their long walks including the West Highland Way and the Pennines. He and his wife have now cut down on their walking since both took up painting.

After further café based refreshments, it was into the city centre to visit Lichfield Cathedral. It is absolutely sensational—darkly Gothic and staggeringly decorated with figure sculptures. The imposing West Front, where the statuary is amazing, reminded me of Rheims or Amiens and the three spires, referred to as 'the ladies of the Vale', give it a dramatic effect. Apparently it is the only English cathedral which still has three spires on its towers. Still reeling from these visionary delights, I ventured inside. The cathedral was started 800 years ago, took 150 years to complete, and was once the shrine of St Chad, its first bishop. After enjoying the lofty simplicity of the nave, I visited the chapel, where St Chad's skull used to be kept, looked at the floor mark where his shrine once stood and then went into the Lady Chapel, where he is presently commemorated. In the Chapter House I saw the priceless Lichfield Gospels— St Matthew, St Mark and part of St Luke—an illuminated manuscript, handwritten in Latin and 1,000 years old. Eight beautifully decorated pages were left, which probably came from Wales. I also noticed an Epstein sculpture of Bishop Woods, 1937-1953, and had a quick look at a numinous exhibition—a series of spiritual works of art in various media by Olwen Ballantine. Quite striking. I left, via the north transept and saw, to one side of the doorway, a fine sculpture of St Chad.

In the Market Place I found the statue of Dr Samuel Johnson, in pensive mood, sculpted by Richard Cockle Lucas and erected in 1838. Not far away was the dandy-ish stone figure of his biographer, James Boswell, by Percy Fitzgerald, erected in 1908.

Having booked and checked into a B & B thanks to the local Tourist Information Centre, I rambled back into town and came to the monument to the captain of the Titanic. He stood on a pedestal with arms crossed, and wearing a captain's hat, long coat and boots. Gerald had told me that the statue was commissioned by Hanley, his home town, but after the sinking they didn't want it. As it was being cast in Lichfield, there it remained.

The sculptor was Lady Kathleen Scott (1878-1947), widow of Captain Robert Falcon Scott (Scott of the Antarctic). One plaque read 'Commander Edward Smith, born January 27, 1850 died April

15th 1912. Bequeathing to his countrymen the memory and example of a great heart, a brave life and heroic death. Be British.'

Then it was onto the Dr Johnson birthplace museum. "Hope you can do the tour in 30 minutes," said the lady custodian, "we close at 4.30." There were paintings, information on Johnson, and quotations from his works: 'Every man is to take existence on the terms on which it is given to him.' I also sat in Johnson's own arm-chair, from Bolt Court, his last London home. There was also a beautifully worded but withering letter by Johnson to his so-called patron, Lord Chesterfield, after the latter stopped funding his dictionary project. One of the pictures that caught my eye was of Erasmus Darwin (1731-1802), grandfather of Charles and another of Lichfield's famous sons. He lived in a house in Beacon Street (1756-1781), near the cathedral, and was author of *The Botanic Garden*. According to the custodian they were thinking of buying a place and opening it as a museum. I completed my city tour with the purchase of a thermal under-vest and *The Staffordshire Way*.

In a pub recommended by the B & B, I had a pint of Old Bailey strong bitter (Mansfield Brewery), a very strong, pleasant taste. Word soon got around, and in the dining room a man eating a huge steak platter said this was the meal I should be having. This proved to be Tony, another B & B guest, who had heard of me from the owner, May. "I admire you. I couldn't do it. I get into the car to get the news-paper," he said. "When May told me you were doing the Land's End-John O'Groats walk I said 'He's resting now,' and she said 'oh no, he's gone to have a look round Lichfield', I couldn't believe it." He asked me lots of questions about my walk, but said that no way would he do anything like it, although he was tall and rangy and looked fit. He asked me if I was writing a book about it. I mentioned I was writing a diary, but the main thing was to actually complete the walk. I returned early to the B & B in order to watch a TV programme on T.E. Lawrence, but I didn't like it very much.

### Wednesday, 30th July
At breakfast Tony checked—"So you don't want a lift anywhere?" I had a long chat with May who came from Birmingham where she

had run a pub. She was offered another in Lichfield, fell in love with the place, and after seven years bought this house and set up a B & B. She was now looking at a much larger house. "I need something to keep me occupied," she said. She also did charity work and was off to keep fit classes.

I left Lichfield around midday and in the late afternoon I stopped at the Drill Inn, a pub that was open all day. It served Cuckoo Ale from the Burton-on-Trent brewery that had a strong hoppy taste. One customer said he knew a man who 12 months ago did the walk in about six or seven weeks "but he was only 30". Beyond Gentleshaw I came to Castle Ring Iron Age hill fort. A sign informed me that 'built around 500 B.C., it is a well preserved hill fort covering nine acres and comprising several ramparts and ditches originally protected by a timber stockade on its main rampart and by massive wooden gates at its entrance. View from fort on highest point of Cannock Chase (760ft) would have given early warning of enemy. The fort would have given scattered farming communities a safe refuge.'

I continued walking through beautiful woods of conifers, birch and beech where I passed two jovial walkers carrying day packs. Would you believe, they had just been talking about the Land's End to John O'Groats walk. It was only a question of time. Not much further on I found a lovely spot to camp—a sheltered clearing in the woods off the track with a stream running by. I was just finishing supper when a man's voice said: "Anyone at home?" I unzipped the front door. "You're not supposed to camp here, you know," he said. "The Foresters don't allow camping. It's a bad area too, I wouldn't leave the tent out of sight." After I told him about my walk, he wanted my advice about equipment, what were the best boots to buy and about the tent. He then re-joined his fellow walkers. I settled down again, thinking that things were going pretty well but that I should be putting in more miles per day. Perhaps I should gradually increase mileage and be more disciplined in walking stages. Later a vehicle stopped close by, and music started coming from the car. Another car arrived later—but both left as I was going to sleep.

*Thursday, 31st July*

The thermal vest certainly helped keep me warm—I can throw away the tattered foil blanket. This morning I could wash in the stream, which was bracing. The day's walk started through lovely forests, picking up a one and a half mile track along which aircraftmen used to carry their kitbags to an RAF base during the Second World War. Alongside, a notice says: 'Land liable to sudden subsidence - keep to path', and further on another says: 'Caution - electric scooters use this road.' It seemed to be a day for notices, for presently I came to a copse commemorated with a plaque by the Burma Star Association: 'This commemorative copse was planted by members of the branch in proud memory of all who fought and died in the Burma campaign 1942-45. When you go home tell them of us and say for your tomorrow we gave our today.'

My next stop proved to be the visitor centre for Cannock Chase. A display informed me about the Community Forest that is proposed to cover 23,000 hectares of southern Staffordshire and Walsall, by planting an area of trees equivalent to 200 football pitches every year for the next 50 years. Not far beyond the visitor centre I came to a memorial, erected by the Anglo-Polish Society: 'In memorial to the 14,000 members of the Polish armed forces who were executed in Katyn Forest in 1940.'

The day was proving damp, the first for some time, and at an anorak putting on stop I also inspected my right foot where the small toe was swollen. I put on some ointment and surgical tape. Not long afterwards I reached the end of the Heart of England Way. I phoned Jenny, then went to the Bull and Mow pub to celebrate, enjoying one of the best pints of the trip so far—King's Champion (Greene King)—a good, biting taste.

So it was on to the Staffordshire Way which I would be following for the next 50 miles—so long as I could interpret the guidebook as it read from north to south. I was soon walking through the grounds of Shugborough, where the quietness was shattered by five jets going overhead, followed by more, then a cyclist whizzing past, then a train. But still lovely woodlands. Then I came to two gate houses, both lived in, then a further gatehouse type and three follies, before reaching Shugborough Hall itself, the ancestral home of Lord Lichfield, the photographer, and now owned by the National Trust. I was too late to look round this massive building with a huge eight column portico, but not to have a tea break in the restaurant. I left over the Essex bridge, the longest packhorse bridge in England, and entered the quaint village of Great Haywood.

The Staffordshire Way now led along the Trent and Mersey Canal. I passed a line of moored narrow boats—in one someone watching TV, in another a semi-naked man was using a portable phone, a family lounged in a third. "Going far?" shouted a man from one just coming in. "Scotland," I replied. Past Colwich Lock I came to the Greyhound, which had a guest beer—Morrells' Graduate. Upon rejoining the Staffordshire Way, it started to rain so I pitched my tent.

### *Friday, 1st August*

August—and a wet day. It started raining, rained on and off all day and was always wet underfoot. At Blithfield Reservoir I decided against following the path as there were too many nettles and it meandered hither and thither, and went direct alongside the reservoir. Walking across a dam at the far end I passed a 'Trespassers will be prosecuted' sign. I'd done it by then, and regained the Staffordshire Way for the last section into Abbots Bromley. An old market butter-cross stood in the village square that dated to the reign of Edward III. The village seemed to be a centre for horn dancers who performed an ancient dance each Wakes Monday in September. A notice in the buttercross said that the reindeer horns which the dancers carry, and that date back to the 11th century, are kept in the parish church. After a part liquid lunch in the Goats Head (Bass this time), I went in search of the horns. I soon found another sign that told me that 'the horn dance was originally performed at the Bartholomew Fair in 1226, and was one of the few ritual rural customs to survive. In its present form, six Deer men, a Fool, Hobby-Horse, Bowman and Maid Marion dance to a Melodeon player at locations throughout the village.' The church duly displayed six reindeer horns and a hobby horse. A woman in the church posed the question as to how the horns

59

arrived in the village. Apparently there is a service in the church when the horns are blessed before being handed over, which raises mixed feelings in the village. It is a pagan ritual but "If it wasn't associated with the church, the other lot would take over," the woman said. "The previous vicar got a bit hot under the collar about it, but I don't know the thinking of the present one. Nowadays we get quite a few witches. They look a bit odd, set themselves up in the school house and sell a few mementos." It turned out she had moved into the village 11 years ago and liked not being in the rat race. "You get a judge living next to a working man—that's nice." In the village I noticed a butcher's shop, so there are some still left.

I left the village in mid-afternoon, as it started to rain once more. The path following the edge of wheat fields, made it hard-going, slow, and even wetter. Once the rain stopped I thought I would try and dry off by walking along the road rather than the Way. After some four miles of road I reached the edge of Uttoxeter and couldn't resist a B & B—my feet were sodden and their skin soggy and crinkly. It was good to wash and dry out.

### Saturday, 2nd August

After a visit to the church that had been largely rebuilt in 1828, I saw the monument in the market square marking the spot where the schoolboy Dr Johnson did penance in 1777 for refusing to help on his father's bookstall. I also hunted for a copy of the South Pennine Way guide, but without success.

Leaving Uttoxeter I became lost on the race course! A helpful man, walking his small dog, put me right—the signs hadn't been put back after the area's redevelopment he explained. But an hour later I was still not out of Uttoxeter—new bridges had replaced old ones, and road works disrupted paths too. I decided I would road walk to Rocester instead. A Little Chef looked appetising but I realised I would have to be frugal from now on, and pound the tarmac to increase progress. At least today was sunny, with just white fluffs of cloud. I soon reached a JCB factory, a long, low building, land-scaped, and unobtrusive. A long time ago I had gone there for an interview for a PR position. "Do you see yourself as a JCB man?" I was asked. I think I took too long to reply, at any rate I didn't get the job. On the other side of road in a field was a JCB statue of a man.

On reaching Denstone I was pondering filling up my water container from a fountain near the cenotaph. An old man, mowing his front lawn, saw me hesitating. "There's nothing wrong with that water," he said. "That's water from the bores. It's never dried up. Gypsies come and fill up milk churns with it." It transpired he was a mine of local history. His stories of the water were supported by the owner of the local shop who said that if a dog was given a choice between tap and fountain water, it would always go for the latter.

The next part of the route lay along a disused railway line in the Churnet Valley. A faint noise in the distance came from Alton Towers. Later on I spotted a Gothic looking castle on a hill, but sewage treatment works rather spoilt the view. At the disused Alton Station, two helpful lads sitting on the platform told me there was the Ramblers Retreat further on and a campsite towards Cotton.

First, however, I went into Alton village and to St Peter's church where I meditated in a chapel with a stained glass window depicting St George and the Dragon. The feeling experienced was quite strong. Then it was into the Bulls Head Inn for bodily refreshment, where I got chatting to a party who had been to Alton Towers for the day. The children tried to play pub skittles but one ball was missing. "Someone nicked it," said the barmaid, "It would cost £100 to replace it."

One of the party asked me "What's next?"

"I don't think there will be a next," I said. She offered to buy me a drink but I said I must go and find myself a nice field to sleep in.

Once I'd reached Oakamoor I realised I had somehow missed the Ramblers' Retreat. I visited the Cricketers for a pint of Cuckoo ale, but felt ill at ease. The customers included several players who had just finished a cricket match, one of whom rudely said: "I've seen everything now, look at that lot," referring to me. Within 20 minutes of leaving the pub I had found a perfect spot to pitch the tent.

*Sunday, 3rd August*

Another cold, fitful sleep. I soon reached the Hawksmoor Nature Reserve, now part of the National Trust, got lost, but soon rejoined the Staffs Way.

At noon I reached Kingsley Holt, but the village shop was closed. In the short time it took to pass a football match along the edge of a field, I saw two goals, and more goals were being scored as I left. I thought it a bit early for football. As I sat by Kingsley War Memorial, still within earshot of the football, a man told me there were a couple of pubs round the corner. I couldn't resist. Of the two I chose the Bull's Head, which had Bass served by an elderly landlord and landlady. Soon the football team turned up. "What was the score?"

"13-0, at least we think it was 13. They had a lot of young players."

With more players piling in, I decided to leave. The Way led through the churchyard, the church itself was closed. But I also became lost in the churchyard, due to the number of kissing gates, but was put right eventually by an old lady walking a dog. The Way soon made a steep descent to the Caldon Canal. At Consall Lock I met up with a retired couple I'd seen last night and who had advised me about the Cricketers Arms. The husband said that if I went up the canal a bit further there was another pub. They love walking. "Got everything here, except the sun," his wife said, "that's why we like going to Cornwall and do the coastal walks." I soon came to the Black Lion and, again, couldn't resist popping in, especially when I saw they sold Titanic beer—it made my day. Good flavour, strong, smooth. Not far beyond the pub the canal kept parallel to the river Churnet and the Way ran between the two. I came across a duck on the towpath trying to eat a fish but it was too big to swallow. Another duck moved in and a fierce squabble ensued.

Further on someone recommended a campsite which I soon found, though it was a one and a half mile hike to a shop for supplies. The campsite owner said my walk was something her husband would like to do. "You're stuck here all the time doing nothing," she said. "I used to be on my feet all day long when I used to work in Leek."

Another woman, talkative, joined in. "You take everything with you, rather like a snail," she observed. Then, "can I ask you a rude question—how old are you?" (Another favourite question was "How are you going to get back from John O'Groats?").

The walk to the shop meant that at least I could go for a varied campsite meal, which I did: tinned mackerel in tomato sauce, potato salad, two bananas and cream, biscuits. Lovely.

## *Monday, 4th August*

Set off along the canal once more to Cheddleton, where a man gave directions to Leek via another canal. After about three-quarters of an hour, the canal stopped to continue as a stream, but a track led on into the market place. Leek has lots of antique shops, but also a bookshop where at long last I could buy a guide to the Pennine Way. I also replenished my cooking gas supply and bought a wool blanket to improve night-time comfort. The two sales ladies were pretty agog about my walk. The youngest said she would have to think about taking up more walking herself. "We always go everywhere by car these days," she said. They asked me to send them a postcard from John O'Groats. Part of the increased weight was compensated for by sending some items back to Jenny's. I then visited the church of St Edward the Confessor, a former national saint of England. It had beautiful stained glass windows including an east window designed by William Morris and Burn-Jones and the north aisle rose window was by the William Morris company.

In the churchyard, one tombstone was of special interest as it recorded the oldest man ever. 'James Robinson - interred Feb the 28th 1788 Aged 438.' It has apparently been mentioned in the *Guinness Book of Records*! But as one of three ladies involved in cleaning the church and who helped me find the tombstone, said: "It's only a silly mistake." It was then time to head on once more, and in late afternoon I reached the village of Rudyard (apparently the name was conferred on a certain Mr Kipling by his parents). I took the opportunity to phone Gill and Brian who were just back from celebrating my Uncle Charles' 90th birthday. Apparently I was the only relation missing—half of them thought I was barmy, the other half courageous.

The route then lay along Rudyard Lake Reservoir to Rushton, and I sat by the lake to eat supper. At the end of the reservoir I met a couple of walkers who advised me of a short cut to the Knot Inn, and though I got lost once, I was soon there. While supping a pint of Boddingtons I asked about camp sites, but the landlord said I could put my tent up behind the pub. As it was now past 8 p.m., overcast and gloomy, it seemed like a good idea. One of the customers, with earrings and short fair hair, was here to work on a nearby canal where a conduit was leaking. He operated a special machine on legs, one of only a few in this country, and was staying at the only B & B for miles around.

### Tuesday 5th August

I'd now completed the Staffordshire Way, and the next section lay along 18 miles of the Gritstone Trail to Lyme Park. I trusted that it would be better waymarked than the Staffordshire Way, as I had no guidebook. But I woke well refreshed to tackle it—oh, the warmth and comfort from my new blanket. What a brilliant buy!

At a garage I got directions from the mechanic, but half an hour later I was lost, for I seemed to be heading south. That was the story of the day—on the Trail one moment, off it the next. But at some, quite early, stage I crossed into Cheshire. Not far beyond the River Dove, I met up with a walker couple. "Never met anyone actually doing the whole walk," said the woman. Both had packs adorned with badges. The husband explained that they were doing a recce for a Ramblers' walk.

Talking of the End to End walk he commented: "Some of our members have done the walk, written about it and got it published."

The route gradually became more exposed, and the wind rose. As I reached Hawkslee Farm there was a panoramic view over Jodrell Bank telescope in the middle of the flat Cheshire Plain. Across the A54 the weather became ever more bracing, more like the 'great out-doors.' I stopped to watch 10 racing pigeons from a nearby farmhouse doing Red Arrow type aerobatics, circling, turning and flying with the wind in formation—terrific.

By late afternoon I had reached the top of Tegg's Nose, with another beautiful view. Beyond was a ridge that led to a visitor centre, but it had closed for the day. Nevertheless, on the viewfinder I saw a pub marked and decided to make for it. Once there I had a pint of Mansfield Classic followed by one of Pedigree, and decided to have a meal too. Not far beyond the pub I picked a spot in a field by a stream to pitch the tent, although the barman had said farmers round here didn't like people camping on their land.

### *Wednesday, 6th August*

During the night I had an odd dream. Animals were coming down a stream towards the tent—mind the guy ropes, don't buck the tent. Then a beast got hold of one of my feet and started biting it. I screamed and tried to struggle free. But I couldn't get free, I couldn't move. Then I woke up.

In Rainow village I once more lost the Gritstone Trail, so asked one man who was leaning against a wall by the war memorial. Despite having lived there 40 years he didn't know where the Trail was. I asked another, elderly chap and he directed me. I soon lost it again, but picked up the signs once more near the top of Kerridge Hill, where White Nancy folly makes a distinctive landmark.

As there had been no shops in Rainow, I made a diversion into Bollington for supplies, a village that nestles in a valley with murky Manchester in the background. I was tempted to stay and have a meal as there were lots of pubs and restaurants, but just dawdled over a pint of Theakston's. The day was very hot, with only a slight breeze, and later I stood on the hillside watching thistle pollen blowing across—like snow flakes floating high and low. At times on, and at others off, the Gritstone Trail I eventually arrived at Lyme Country Park to find the café closed—the story of my life, just missed it.

I celebrated the end of the Gritstone Trail with an apple and some water sitting by a pond. But I felt a bit deflated—why is it that the National Trust, who own Lyme Park, have to close it at 5 p.m., it's a typically English closing time. I watched youngsters paddling in the pond, and an Indian family playing football. Leaving the park, I had to ask three sets of people before getting a direction to the Macclesfield Canal. After another pub stop I hunted for a field camping spot when I spied a farmer. He was a big, brawny, bearded man, and he agreed quite happily to my camping in one of his fields. Tomorrow should be the last stretch before reaching the Pennine Way near Crowden. I could have joined the Way at Edale, the usual starting point, but my guidebook strongly recommended avoiding the first part which has been heavily eroded.

### *Thursday, 7th August*

As I breakfasted, I told myself: "Don't be intimidated by the prospect of the Pennine Way. Look forward to enjoying it as much as rest of journey." The day was hot and sunny, the aim Crowden and my junction with the Pennines.

Whilst enjoying an ice cream in Compstall, I chatted to an elderly man. "There was a young man through here last week, aged about 28 with a placard on his back, doing the walk for some charity." In Etherow Country Park I went into the visitor centre to check my day's route, then took advantage of the adjacent café. As the day wore on I gradually closed on the Pennines. They looked very barren and remote, forbidding almost.

In Hadfield I met an elderly male walker who said there was an excellent camp site at Crowden, and he gave me directions. I decided to pause for an afternoon pint, Robinson's best bitter in the Palatine pub, then set off along the Longdendale track, a disused railway line, alongside a reservoir for Crowden. I became confused as to when I was actually in Crowden, but then realised I'd reached a Pennine Way marker, found the campsite and pitched my tent.

# 5. Pennine Way South

*Friday, 8th August*

It was a noisy night. The warden told me one family left at the crack of dawn—apparently the children were being bitten by midges and couldn't sleep. As the gates didn't technically open till 7 a.m., they had left the car by the warden's caravan with the engine running till they were let out. No wonder I couldn't sleep!

It felt good to be on the Pennine Way at last and to see the signs with the acorn. I passed a young male walker going in the opposite direction. "Black Hill? It's dry and spongy, no trouble," he said. "Just take it at your own pace. From the top there is a beautiful view looking towards the Crowden valley and river." But the flies were irritating—were they the same ones or were they continually changing, renewing? I followed a sedgy, red-coloured stream then miles of paving stones made the walking easier. Reaching a cairn and looking round I could see exactly how you could get lost—it's a flat landscape with no landmarks, only sheep. Eventually I gained the top of the notorious Black Hill, usually an unnegotiable quagmire. But there was no mud today, thank goodness, and I trekked across the crusty earth to reach the Trig point at its centre. Following directional cairns down the other side of Black Hill I noted how badly eroded the paths are with isolated grass tufts sticking in lonely solitude out of the earth. Beyond Wessenden Reservoir I became confused as to the

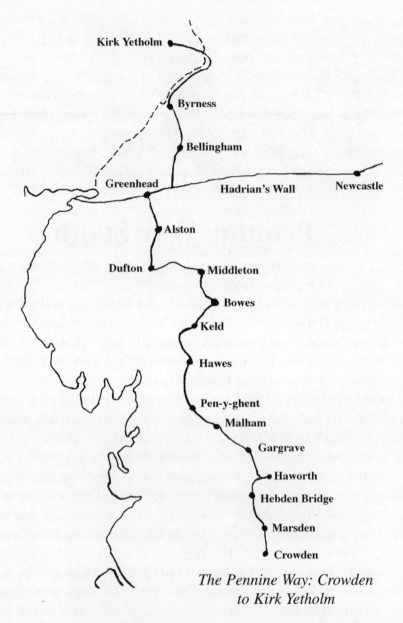

*The Pennine Way: Crowden*
*to Kirk Yetholm*

route once more. It took me an hour to realise I was on the wrong map page, although it did look similar. Finally I got back on the right track—and into a swarm of flying ants waiting to take off. Minutes later they were airborne!

On the outskirts of Marsden I realised I was going the wrong way again. Too bad! A man told me of a good B & B, and even took me there. A knock on the door was answered by a man about to have a bath, who said he would check with his wife, when she had returned from a Chinese takeaway. So I left my rucksack and went to a nearby pub that he recommended and which had its own brewery. The Riverhead Brewery Tap had several beers, all excellent and whilst I supped their March Haigh Special, first a black dog called Guinness came in, then four boys on roller blades. Gradually the pub filled with lots of interesting characters. I was joined by the B & B man who brought the keys to my room and I booked in.

### Saturday, 9th August

I couldn't get to sleep for a long time, as there was not much air and I was suffering from insect bites on my legs and feet (how—through two pairs of socks?), face, neck and both hands and arms. I treated the bites with TCP.

When I asked, over breakfast, about a family portrait of the landlady, her mother, daughter and grand-daughter, it made Kath, the landlady, tearful. It turned out her mother had only died in April, and they were still to bury her ashes in the garden. "Mother had lived with us for 20 years. I have three lovely grand-children to help make up for the loss. Now I'll concentrate more on the B & B. I've got to keep busy somehow."

As I tried to get in to St Bartholomew's parish church, a car drove up. The driver, who turned out to be the organist, let me in and kindly told me something of its history. "The church was locked because we've had burglaries, the lot. It was left open for 10 minutes once and vandals came in." The present church was built in 1890 with money from the Whitehead family who owned a building company. It had lovely stained glass windows, including three modern ones by Leonard Walker with rich, yet subdued colours. "It was previously a chapel—the floor was of earth so the people could have the privilege of being buried within its walls. But eventually all the available space was taken up, many of the bodies being only a few inches below the surface. The then incumbent, who set the new building in motion, reputedly said that the building was in a thoroughly insanitary condition, it being literally crammed with dead bodies. The estimated cost was £10,000."

The road out of the village was lined with sheep. At lunchtime I popped into Ward's Great Western and tried Waggle Dance—'brewed with pure honey - strong, smooth and delicious', according to Vaux Brewers. It tasted sweetish, but nice and moorish. Lovely after-taste. Working my way through the other beers I commented about the sheep on the road. The landlord told me that motorists are liable to pay for any sheep they run over—the farmers say the sheep were here before the cars. I stayed on for food and another beer. "We have a customer who comes in Friday and Saturday night and has a few Waggle Dances and goes out in a rum state." A beer mat explains that Waggle Dance was 'named after the dance performed by bees as a way of indicating distant nectar sources to their companions.' I dragged myself away and back to the Pennine Way again. Granite rocks, peat bogs, dry and spongy, and a good path made for good fast walking. I noticed cotton plants with fluffy white bolls. Although a hot sunny day, there was a nice breeze. Coming onto the A672, a large gaggle of Indians, in safaris and traditional dress, passed me and asked "Is it a good view?" I crossed the M62 on a special walkers' bridge, the path itself being a very noticeable scar through the countryside. As I rambled I recalled a book called *Jupiter* about a round-the-world motor-cyclist. The author made the point that it was the everyday way of life that appealed to him rather than the objective of getting somewhere.

Later I managed to walk past the White House pub without stopping—but then it was closed! I found a good spot just off the main path near a craggy outcrop of rock with magnificent views to pitch the tent. The bites on my legs were now a livid red—goodness knows what insect was responsible. In addition the dreaded midges were back again.

### Sunday, 10th August

When I awoke I looked outside, into low, misty cloud, visibility poor, and it was windy. What a change from yesterday. I enjoyed a deep meditation, only slightly marred by the distant sound of a hunting horn and hounds. The path had been heavily eroded and the surface repaired with slabs. I could just make out Stoodley Pike monument to the north-east. As I headed towards it I first passed a solid high-backed stone seat with a plaque: 'This seat was built in memory of our dad Cyril Webster who died Dec 1992. Still walking the hills.' Then I passed the point where the Pennine Way crosses the Calderdale Way, a 50-mile circular route, and eventually reached Stoodley Pike, a massive millstone construction. A plaque reads: 'Erected by public subscription to commemorate surrender of Paris to the Allies and finished after battle of Waterloo when peace was established in 1815. By a strange coincidence the pike fell on the day the Russian Ambassador left London before declaration of [the Crimea] war with Russia. Was rebuilt when peace was restored in 1856.' As I dawdled near the structure I overheard two walkers: "Mary was struggling up the hill," a woman said. "What with those legs?" a man responded.

As I neared Hebden Bridge, the land became flatter and enclosed fields replaced moorland, and I entered the town along a canal towpath. The town was busy and had lots of 'watering-holes' to choose from. I chose the White Lion Hotel, where the barman let me taste the beer first. Then I supped pints of Cain's (Liverpool) and Castle Eden (Durham). The Bridge Café supplied lunch, topped off with ice cream. Stocking up on supplies, a shop owner quoted Wainwright as saying "I got off the Pennine Way with relief, the Cross Country Way with regret."

The mist had now totally lifted, the day was hot, but storms threatened. Near a railway tunnel, a small boy asked whether I would like a drink of water. He lived nearby and his mother looked apprehensively over her paper. By 5.30 p.m. I was up on the hills again after a steep climb. Through narrow walled paths and down another steep hill, I came across four lads swimming in a pool. "I wanted to go skinny-dipping," said one. "My bollocks, oh," said another, wading. On the far side I found a road and the rough and ready New Delight pub. As I waded through Morland's Old Speckled Hen (strong with bitter taste, light colour), and Deakins (nice drop), I asked the barmaid about using the camping facilities at the back of the pub. She replied:

"I think it'll be all right, but ask the landlady", pointing to a woman sitting in the corner, smoking and drinking a pint. It was, so I continued my beverage tour with Mansfield bitter (nice colour). I started to feel well oiled, but lonely. Perhaps it was the juke box playing songs like Buffalo Bill and Don McLean's haunting 'Vincent'. I erected the tent, solitary in a large sloping field at the back of the pub but was presently joined by a big family with noisy children that pitched four tents next to mine. Perhaps I should be better lonely, but after my meal I returned to the pub for a coffee and Martell brandy. Outside, a party was going on with music from the car tape recorder. "Come and join us," a woman shouted. I declined.

### *Monday, 11th August*

What a night! I didn't drop off until 2.30 a.m. when the family fell asleep. At 10.30 p.m. they had started a barbecue. Andy, a scout-master it turned out, did the cooking. He told the kids to be quiet but it didn't make much difference, and I could hear their conversation. Mark, to his sisters: "You don't know what getting up is about. I have to get up at 5 a.m. to do my paper round." He had a telescope and was looking at the stars. They all joined in and there were lots of 'oohs' and 'ahs' when they saw a shooting star. When the adults returned from the pub, drunk, they too gazed at the stars and nattered aimlessly about cosmology. When that topic quickly petered out they took to singing songs—loudly. At just after 7 a.m. I was woken by Mark suddenly yelling "What's the time, why didn't you wake me?" Terry: "I did several times." He went off to walk four miles to work.

When I finally arose over two hours later I noticed some of the bites on my feet and ankles were now like boils. How did this happen? The weather was now sultry and overcast and crossing the moor, black evil-looking flies were hovering about—could they be the villains. I was soon walking through swarms of these insects, but didn't think that they stung. I had to keep my mouth shut or blow out, to prevent receiving a mouthful of the creatures and their long black legs. At lunchtime I reached Top Withens along slabs over the moor. A ruined farmhouse bore the sign: 'This farmhouse has been associ-ated with *Wuthering Heights*, the Earnshaw home in Emily Bronte's novel. The building, even when complete, bore no resemblance to the house she described. But the situation may have been in her mind when she wrote of the moorland setting of the Heights." This plaque had been placed here by the Bronte Society in response to many enquiries. I chatted to two walkers doing the Pennine Way, one of whom said he had seen me—"this old man with a white hat"—the day before. "You must be one in a million," he said, when I told him of my walk. "You wait until I tell the wife, she's only 26, that this old man is walking 1,000 miles." Less of the old, I thought. He had also met a man doing the End to End the other way who was living rough all the time and surviving mainly on porridge. Leaving the ruin I met a gnarled old man, brown as a nut, with an ancient bicycle. "I'm 70, not feeling too well. Come to see the house where Heathcliff lived, didn't he? Do you know anything about medicine?" Once past a signpost, written in both English and Japanese, I left the Pennine Way to go to Haworth—I wanted to visit the Bronte Museum and also needed a B & B so I could wash some clothes.

Having successfully found a B & B that would undertake such a chore on my behalf, I had a hot bath, washed my hair and treated my bites. I felt brilliant as a result. A leaflet in the B & B informed me that the Irish born Rev. Patrick Bronte came to live at Haworth parsonage in 1820 with his Cornish wife Maria and their six young children, Maria, Elizabeth, Charlotte, Branwell, Emily and Anne.

After sampling Fat Rascal, Yorkshire Parkin and Yorkshire curd tart in an air-conditioned café, my next port of call was the Fleece Inn, a traditional pub that had a Happy Hour with all six Timothy Taylor ales brewed in Keighley at 99p a pint. I could manage three— Ram Tam (dark, strong old beer), Porter (sweet, dark, malty stout), and Landlord (a classic pale ale). Another inn offered Webster's beers and more food.

### Tuesday, 12th August

At breakfast I met a Japanese family staying at the B & B—it was part of their literary education to visit Haworth. The landlady said one Japanese stayed three days and every day he went to the Parsonage museum. I visited the church of St. Michael and All Angels, just 100 years old, for the old church was demolished in the teeth of strong opposition from a combination of antiquarians and Bronte lovers, but the deteriorating condition of graves under the old building brought matters to a head. 40,000 villagers are reputedly buried in the grave-yard. Thence my own pilgrimage to the Parsonage museum. Apparently the Rev. Patrick changed his name from Pounty or Bounty to Bronte in imitation of Nelson who had become Duke of Bronte.

It was only an hour's walk before I could fall into the Wuthering Heights pub in Stanbury and have a pint of Gooseye—only it wasn't. The landlord subsequently realised he had connected the wrong pipes, and I was actually drinking Ridleys. "I don't know whether I'm coming or going," he said. But the beer was not good—end of the barrel, so I tried an actual pint of Gooseye, but it had a distinc-tive taste—too sharp and not to my taste.

By early afternoon I was back on the Pennine Way. I then came across an unsavoury old man wearing a raincoat and cloth cap lying on the path, with one eye nearly closed and two cuts on his mouth. "When you're our age you've got to keep walking," he said. "Be careful what you sleep on. You can get rheumatism very easily. I've been walking all my life and I'm not 60 yet." (He looked much older.)

Later I passed two girl walkers. "Don't envy you climbing the hill," said one. "People have been collapsing up there." Nevertheless, I made it—with a grand view south of the reservoir and in the distance numerous wind generators. The Way then led along a slab path across a rather desolate heather moor. I passed several chalets, presumably for shooters, some with little chimneys. Conveniently I reached Cowling at 6 p.m. and walked straight into the Black Bull for a pint of Tetley's. A group of walkers doing the Way north to south arrived and ordered four pints of Coca Cola and beef crisps. They'd been averaging 20 miles a day! The landlord, Dick, came in and persuaded me to take a room for £10. "Don't nick the toilet paper and leave my razor alone," he joked as he showed me my very basic room. The night was not good—the room overlooked the A6508 with vehicles echoing as they went past, whilst the juke box down below pounded away. I felt guilty, for I shouldn't be staying at another B & B and drinking and eating so much and wasting money. I felt depressed, too, perhaps because I'd only covered about seven miles in five hours. Not a good day all in all.

### Wednesday, 13th August

The day dawned overcast and cooler, if clammy. Rain came on for a while, and spotted during the day. It was a day for solid plodding and catching up on distance—following lots of drystone walling to Thornton-in-Craven where I paused for only a quick look. Later the route followed the Leeds and Liverpool Canal and I did pause at the Abbot's Harbour tea-house by a canal bridge. The owners used the building's connection with monks and nuns in every way they could think. I ordered a Friar's Seduction (I could have had a Friar's Passion), a special apple slice with sweet caramel on top, and found I was sitting at Novice Nathan's table. On a nearby table was a notice 'For visiting nuns'.

In late afternoon I reached Gargrave and went to visit St Andrews Church. The vicar, just leaving, let me in. "We usually keep it open and lock it at night. I'll come back later and lock it." I discovered that Iain MacLeod MP, briefly Chancellor of the Exchequer in 1971, is buried in the churchyard.

On leaving I found that one pub at least was open, but the beer was not kept well, though I learnt where the campsite was. Later I found the Old Swan that had Abbot Ale, but the pub quickly filled with people wanting to watch Newcastle play Croatia at football. I left, but felt better as in eight hours walking, I had covered 12 miles.

### Thursday, 14th August

Whilst breakfasting, an elderly back-packer, in shorts, and pugilistic looking, came over and gave me several small packets of cereal and dried milk. He said he was going home and wouldn't need them. Very nice of him.

The walking started with easy going through fields, and then by the River Aire, only I should have been heading north, not west, and should have paid more attention to the map. I was corrected by a young couple, also walking to Malham. I made Malham by lunchtime, and in the Buck Inn I had a couple of pints of Black

Sheep, brewed next to Theakston at Masham. From the village to the Cove is a patchwork of walls. The Cove itself is a unique exposure of the Great Scar Limestone at the Mid-Craven fault, standing 80m high and 300m wide. Outstanding. As I approached I passed a woman walking a dog which started yapping at me. "Dogs don't like my rucksack," I said.

"It's not that, she doesn't like men," came the retort.

A steep ascent brings you to the crest and an amazing limestone pavement. It's full of ridges and clefts known as clints and grikes—and quite a few tourists. The sun had once again broken through and the air was crystal clear as I followed a path through barren, glacial type scenery toward Malham Tarn nature reserve. It seemed cooler walking close to this fair sized lake. The reserve, apparently of international importance, is owned by the National Trust. The path then led into high moors off the road and I decided to pitch camp. I felt tired, especially having just passed a young man going the other way,who'd done 27 miles in 12 hours. It depressed me!

As I cooked and ate my meal I resolved to drink less beer, walk further each day and stop at fewer B & Bs. Meeting the young man would perhaps act as a stimulus.

*Friday 15th August*

During the morning's walk I had a sudden seizure as I bent down to pick up my rucksack after a pit-stop. I felt I couldn't stand up straight and had a sudden feeling of panic. I hoped it was okay and it seemed to be so. A rocky path made a steep descent with a good view of Pen-y-ghent (694m), the next major climb. On the way up an hour later a man said "There's a young man enjoying himself", referring to me and my sack.

The top of Pen-y-ghent held lots of other walkers. I lay on the grass awhile soaking up the sunshine and magnificent view. It's panoramic, unbelievably beautiful, with nothing but moors stretching for miles, plus clouds and sky. One of the 'high spots' so far. Coming off the peak I passed two guys with pick-axes and shovels, continuing the flight of stone steps. "Looks a tough job," I said.

"We've had worse," said one. I thanked them both for their efforts.

I used Horton in Ribblesdale to stock up on supplies, then called in at the walker's café, which also has books and equipment on sale. As I headed off I spotted the Crown Inn, where several people sat outside drinking and, despite my previous night's pledge, I couldn't resist. I had a pint of Theakston's Old Peculier, which looks like treacle, tastes like a strong stout and smells like Bisto, but is very good and in a class of its own. It also left a lovely after taste—it was a beer and a half.

The Way then led along a green track by stone walls and made for fast walking. Past Old Ing farm I followed another pack horse track, and soon rested by a stream which disappears into a big hole in the ground. The water tumbles down 50 to 100ft or more. Not much further on I passed an old barn in a field of lush grass, and decided it was too good to miss. I put up the tent with lovely views across moors to the peaks of Ingleborough and Whernside. I congratulated myself that I had travelled for nine hours and walked about 14 miles.

### Saturday, 16th August

It was a warm night and difficult to sleep, followed by another blisteringly hot day, but at least there was a breeze. For the first two hours I hardly saw anyone, but then my seclusion was shattered, first by a group of 20 or more cyclists in gaudy gear taking up the whole track. "How do" and "all right" they ventured. Then two motorcyclists overtook me, followed by a Range Rover and a Royal Mail van going to a farm, and finally a third motorcyclist. The van stopped on the way back and a bearded, tanned face peered out of the window. "Warm enough for you? Hawes is only two hours away, all downhill. Expect it's a bit too warm." It took me a full two hours to come sufficiently over the brow of the hill to even see Hawes in the valley below.

I came to a field with a 'Bull in pasture' sign, but the animal was in the bottom far corner and not interested in me in the slightest. Further on another gaggle of mountain bikers, of all ages, were going up. There were lots of butterflies. Then Wensleydale Dairy Products with its visitors' centre suddenly came in sight. I went in, joined a tasting queue and was soon enjoying small wedges of 12 or more different cheeses, including ginger, apricot, chives, cranberry, smoked, mature. I bought a piece of ginger cheese for supper, and Brymor real dairy ice cream for now. Leaving, I noticed that the workers, all in white including white Wellington boots, were taking time off in the hot sunshine. They looked the same pale colour as the cheese. A brochure told me that the first real Wensleydale cheese was made by Cistercian monks who settled here in 1150. This was followed by farmhouse cheesemaking after the Reformation, and the first commercial creamery was founded in 1897. The company got into financial trouble but was rescued by Kit Calvert MBE, a dalesman, and is now making 750 tons of cheese a year by traditional methods.

In Hawes itself I had a quick look at St Margaret's Church and then found myself in the Fountain Hotel for a pint each of John Smith and Theakston's best. Drawing money from the bank, I realised how little I had left. So I phoned Jenny, and she agreed to lend me £500. That should be enough to last me until I reached John O'Groats. But how wonderful. I celebrated with a large lunch at Laura's Cottage café. It seemed a particularly hot afternoon and evening, so I booked into the Bainbridge and Ing caravan site that had been recommended by walkers I'd passed. It was virtually full. A young German couple on a tandem with a trailer and flag with BOB on it pitched their tent near mine. The male said: "Going to the pub, I suppose!" as I was leaving. Too true! The White Hart Inn sold Black Sheep and Webster's, though the craggy-faced old barman advised me not to have Webster's. "Very soft, only a couple of people drink it. Don't know why we keep it." Then it was onto The Crown for a pint of Theakston's Old Peculier. I felt much better now in the knowledge of £500 going into the bank, but quite drunk after the Old Peculier. It was just as well the Herriott Hotel I passed on my way back to the campsite didn't serve non-residents.

### Sunday, 17th August

Felt lazy, but spurred myself on the few miles to Hardraw, famous for its waterfall, the only entrance to which is through the Green Dragon Inn. A small fee is payable. The waterfall, set in an amphitheatre of rock, looked impressive, although it was not in full flow. With my eyes, I followed the cascade of water from the top down to the bottom. Looking at the waterfall in this way, the water seems to be slowed down, but it made me feel quite giddy. Leaving Hardraw the Way led up into the moors again. As on many previous days, the sun started to break through and the temperature rose. I sat down to lunch when four auto-cross riders, in gaudy gear, helmets and goggles, went noisily past. But there was a magnificent view that included Ingleborough and Hawes.

The part of the Way to the top of Great Shunner Fell is badly eroded with flagstones used for long stretches. How on earth did they get all these flagstones up here and in place, I wonder. The view was truly superb—panoramic, breathtaking. It was a pity about a nearby fence, otherwise it is a wild and remote spot. Once over the brow I could see Thwaite below in more friendly looking countryside, and an hour later I was in the town, taking the opportunity of a café stop. Back up on a heather clad hill above, I compared camping notes with a ginger-haired man carrying a big sack like mine. He had been walking for a week so far, travelling the Pennine Way from north to south. As the afternoon wore on there was a brilliant light, pure as crystal. Soon I was following a shallow river bed, the Swale, to a campsite in Keld, shopless, publess Keld. I calculated I had walked 12 miles in nine hours, so a good day. And no pub to tempt me.

### Monday, 18th August

Awoke to find a tent had even been erected in the churchyard—a bit spooky, I would have thought. Especially with a bright, full moon. The morning's climb was hot and sticky. There was no breeze. No noise. Just insects. But as it levelled out, I revived, and particularly when I could see the Tan Hill Inn ahead. It is reputed to be the highest pub in the country at 1,732ft above sea level. A pub has been on the site for hundreds of years, which was an important cross-roads for drovers herding cattle to markets and farms in northern England. I ordered a pint of Theakston's XB, then one of Old Peculier. I had a snack to help soak up some of the alcohol, but left feeling slightly inebriated. The afternoon seemed full of grouse, especially with so little else to look at. It is almost impossible to think there is so much empty space—it is flat, bleak, nothing. There is a road to the east, however, whilst it was good to see boot marks on the track. Two more grouse made a croaking noise, followed by more grouse. Incredibly remote, just heather and bog. It became much cooler as I continued to disturb grouse and entered County Durham. There is just a nothingness around—except for black flies everywhere which now rejoined grouse as features in the landscape. Then come grouse hides, with grouse popping up in all directions. At one pit stop I could see long grouse necks peering out of grass, but they weren't disturbed when I clapped my hands. I must have been over-concentrating on grouse for I realised I'd lost the track. Then I spotted three male walkers ahead on the same line and appreciated that they and the path were heading to Bowes. Having lost sight of them later, I tried to change direction onto a disused, overgrown rail track, but it petered out and I was forced onto the A66. I managed to get off the A road and onto another rail track, duly ending up in Bowes where I found a central campsite.

In the evening I went to look at Bowes Castle. It stands within the north-west corner of a Roman Fort which commanded the road from York to Carlisle. A plaque read: 'It came into the possession of the crown in 1171, after which the present keep was probably built, serving in the wars against Scotland. By 1341, the castle was badly in need of repair and of little use, and is thought to have been dismantled and stripped of much of its stone face in 17th century.' Another visitor, looking at the fields immediately behind the castle and church, said it reminded him of his youth in Cornwall; there was something about being close to the elements. Then I succumbed once more and entered the Ancient Unicorn Inn for a pint of Theakston's, again accompanied by food. The food came in enormous portions, the size of which staggered a French family. I didn't feel at all sociable for some reason. Five guys I'd spoken to before were in the pub, but I ignored them. It made me think of the film, Groundhog Day, when time was turned back and the action so to speak was replayed. Perhaps I should do the same. Near the campsite is Dotheboys Hall immortalised, I discovered, by Charles Dickens in Nicholas Nickleby. It's a large, square-shaped red-brick building, currently up for sale.

# 6.  Pennine Way North

*Tuesday, 19th August*

Next came the northern stage of the Pennine Way, a further 130 miles. As I prepared to leave I met the three Musketeers from yesterday (those I'd partially followed into Bowes), jolly, happy, singing. One guy said that if he won the Lottery he would go with his rucksack on a walk like mine. I went into the Post Office/general store where a friendly lady sorted out cash for me. "I love running this place," she said. "I was doing it for two years when the post mistress was taken ill with cancer and in February I took over the rent. It's lovely meeting everyone."

My chosen route led along a road past signs with 'MOD danger - poisonous gas area. Keep out.' I saw the foundations of old Air Ministry buildings and later came across hundreds of empty cartridge cases in a small clearing by a marshy bit. Even further on were MOD firing range danger notices. The Way led across moorland—it struck me as amazing how much land there is. Little greeny brown birds in reeds suddenly took off, while Swaledale sheep abounded. The outcrops of Goldsborough gritstone on Cotherstone Moor are like giant stone books with the layers of gritstone as pages. Later I had a rest by the side of Blackton Reservoir, having walked along a road accompanied by a gaggle of cyclists including several children. I soon reached Middleton, reflecting that the day had been a pleasant walk, certainly in comparison with the previous day which had been a bit intimidating. There was a campsite in town, which I chose, and used the site's bar and restaurant before exploring the town's hostelries.

In the Bridge Inn I met the three walkers once more and we compared notes. They had got lost and hadn't enjoyed the day so much. They came from the Manchester area, two of them going as far as Alston and Steve to the end of the Pennine Way. We moved on to the Teesdale Hotel where they kindly bought me a pint of Teesdale bitter (High Force Hotel Brewery), with its excellent, hoppy taste. They couldn't get over my lack of planning.

### Wednesday, 20th August

The day began with easy walking in meadows near Teesdale River, and when I had a pit stop, the three guys went past me. "We decided to go before the pubs opened." Further on I passed them as they rested by the tree-lined river. The river became faster flowing and through rocks as I reached Low Force waterfall. Canoeists were coming through the rapids, and with the melodic noise of the water I could have stayed all day. But I pulled myself away and entered meadows full of flowers. It is a National Nature Reserve, rising to over 2,500ft, famous for its 'Teesdale Assemblage', a community of plants found only here. A touch later, walking through juniper bushes, I suddenly came to High Force waterfall, in all her majesty. Water is spewed out, brown coloured and angry looking, and the noise is thunderous. From the top, the water is even browner and more turbulent, and I chose to sit by the gorge and have my lunch. Most trippers were on the other bank, where I could see the German tandem couple. Not long after I'd set off once more the trio passed me again. I presently crossed the river and found a little mouse trying to hide in grass, and managed to stroke it. Further on I caught up with the trio, but we parted at Saur Hill Bridge as they were leaving the Way to go to a youth hostel at Langdon Beck. As the afternoon wore on it started to rain, and crossing glistening boulders along the edge, I slipped and fell, nearly going into the water. When I reached Cauldron Snout, another waterfall where the river gushes through rock, I decided to pitch the tent. It was still raining and it looked bleak, but once the tent was up and I'd made a cup of tea, I felt better. Indeed, the weather cleared up and I appreciated that I couldn't have picked a better spot, with river, waterfall and rocks. The man who had given me the cereals several days back had said "Give my regards to Teesdale." I knew what he meant now.

### Thursday, 21st August

I enjoyed one of my best meditation programmes so far this trip. It even included the 'flying' sidhi, confined to a static hopping up and down. This morning I was looking forward to reaching the scenic highlight of High Cup, a massive steep basin plunging down to the Eden Valley. But it started raining as I packed up ready to leave and was pouring as I scrambled up rocks to the top of Cauldron Snout, which more than lives up to its reputation. It really does explode out of the rock, brown, angry and noisy. Beyond lay a concrete dam wall, my way continuing past the dam and Cow Green Reservoir and crossing the Tees into Cumbria. Through a farmyard the route became a boggy uphill slog. I noticed two walkers behind and felt relatively safe, for the track was getting worse and the rain more severe. But when I looked behind again they weren't there any more—they were on the other side of Maize Beck. I retraced my steps and scrambled across the rain swollen beck to the other side. The terrain was bleak and the rain now torrential. I took off my glasses to see better, for they were steamed up and wet, but it made little difference for visibility was down to a few yards. Though I couldn't see the other two walkers, I was following a clear trail, with cairns and markers. When I reached High Cup Gill I bumped into them and they told me Dufton, my intended destination, was to my right. "We only came for the view," one said. Then, pointing at the fog, "Have you got any last words?"

"Say I lived a happy life. I went out with a bang. Perhaps a parachute would come in useful." We all laughed. I squelched on, my boots full of water. The path petered out at a gate marked 'Private'. I tried to relocate myself but couldn't find the right map page (I kept them loose in my map folder, which was leaking). I attempted to go down a wire fence, clinging tightly to the posts. Then I thought I saw a path and started going diagonally towards it. It was very steep and I was getting nervous, before I realised it wasn't a path at all. I had to go back, clinging on for dear life, to the top. Feeling exhausted and hungry I ate some dates and decided I'd better go back. I was wandering along the original path, wondering what to do when out of the mist emerged two walkers that I had met briefly two days previously. After going a bit further along my old path, the taller one called George took out a portable satellite navigation set. I couldn't believe it as he linked up to three satellites and fixed our position to within 50 yards. It was still pouring down, visibility practically nil, but we eventually came to the track leading down and soon the mist lifted and we could see the Eden Valley below us—and Dufton.

When Bow Hall Farm appeared with a B & B sign and another for tea and coffee, we scampered in like three drowned rats and were soon enjoying hot beverages. I certainly needed mine, I was all in. George was taking penicillin tablets with his. Chatting with them, it transpired that George, Scottish, went to Edinburgh University, had lived in Canada, and now lives in Weybridge, while his companion, David, had a broken nose, laughed frequently, repeated things, and wore an Australian type hat. They go walking together, particularly in southern France. They had walked the first stage of the Way before and had just begun the second half at Tan Hill. George said his GIS machine cost about £200; it used batteries pretty quickly so he only turned it on when necessary to get a bearing. As the landlady of the B & B, Sarah, wasn't fussy about wet clothes and dirty boots, I decided to stay. "My mother used to fuss a lot about the housework, but I don't," she said. The other two, pre-booked into the Dufton pub, left. I relished a really hot bath, which was followed by dinner. It seemed light years away from the morning. It was an interesting experience but could have been dangerous, and I would have to take extra precautions in future. Whilst it was a big disappointment not being able to see the spectacular view from High Cup, supposed to be one of the best on the whole route, I was glad to be safe, well-fed and warm. On BBC's North News there was a piece about the fire danger on the Yorkshire Dales—not much chance of that today!

### Friday, 22nd August

What a difference a day makes! The morning dawned lovely blue skies and sunny. The track from the village, full of puddles from yesterday's rain was along an old overgrown, sunken path that later passed the deserted Halsted farm. To the west, as I climbed, I could see practically the whole range of Lake District mountains, and back across the Eden Valley. Around lunchtime I reached Knock Fell, with a great square of stones on top, and further on a teetering cairn. Reaching the top of Great Dun Fell (848m) it felt like being on top of the world, though marred by radio masts and domes. From here the route was flag-stoned to Little Dun with beyond the inhospitable Cross Fell, the highest point of the Pennine Way at 893m. In between lay brown earthworks, with diggers at work. Nearing Cross Fell the terrain was very exposed and it was reassuring to see footprints in the peat bogs. The top was desolate, almost like a lunar or glacial landscape though there were, of course, lots of sheep. Walking round the shelter, admiring the northern part of the Lake District mountains, I was surprised to find a man eating biscuits. "You can see all the pollution in the air," he said. "That blue haze over there," pointing towards the Lakes "is polluted. I tried to come up here three weeks ago, but the weather was so bad that I had to turn back. I couldn't see the cairns." Now we could see the Solway Firth estuary by Carlisle. Two girl walkers passed coming the other way—the place was getting downright crowded!

The route then followed a corpse trail, along which coffins used to be transported, to Greg's Hut. This cottage was restored by the Mountain Bothies Association and a couple of moutaineering and ski clubs in memory of John Gregory who died in a climbing accident in 1968. His friend, Bob Broxap, who tried to save him, later died in a canoeing accident despite the efforts of his canoeing partner. The hut contained chairs and benches, had an open fire place and a very black kettle, and another room with an old collapsing metal bed. In the late afternoon I was on my way again, seeing nothing but sheep, though I could hear grouse and make out what looked to be shooting hides, nine in all. Eventually I could spot my destination, the village of Garrigill, tucked away in a hollow. There was tremendous clarity, with the air very still and quiet—if filling with midges. As I arrived in the village and headed towards the George and Dragon, a voice called out: "Are you Tony? Three guys, who've gone on to Alston, said you were doing the Land's End to John O' Groats walk. So am I. My name is Nicky." It was brilliant to meet another End to Ender. We went into the pub and we sat and talked about our different experiences. She had started in May, first walking from Torbay, where she lives, to Land's End. She had taken three weeks out while her mother was on holiday and had just rejoined the walk at Hawes. She had a light-weight tent and was trying to do 15-20 miles a day. She was tall, with a mop of thick light brown hair, spoke with a soft Devon accent, and was reading John Paul Sartre's *Nausea*. It transpired she used to work for Campervan and had travelled the country, visiting the major cities.

In the dark we left the pub and walked the half mile to where Nicky was camped. She held a torch while I put up my tent, and then we looked at the stars, she pointing out the Plough and North Star.

### *Saturday, 23rd August*

Nicky was off and away whilst I was still shaving—we agreed to leave notes at John O' Groats if we didn't see each other *en route*. It was raining when I left, and raining when I reached Alston, England's highest market town. Walking up the street an elderly man said: "Are you going the whole way? I was told there was someone." He introduced himself as Ken who was walking the other way, but not doing it religiously. So we popped into a pub, the quaint looking 17th century Angel Inn, for a chat. Ken, now living near Land's End and a young-looking 74 year-old, was a member of the Long Distance Walkers' Association and was studying an Open University course, to "learn some culture." He was walking in trainers, and carried just a bivvie bag instead of a tent. We shook hands as he went back to the youth hostel. It was still raining, so I visited St Augustine's parish church. I learnt from the church history that 'at the turn of the century Alston's population was over 10,000 (compared to 1,400 today), lying, as it did, at the heart of the world's largest lead producing area.' In the past the Quaker controlled London Lead Company developed the lead mines at nearby Nenthead and was considered a model company for its enlightened attitude to its workers' welfare.

Although still raining I wanted to get on, and so set off once more. A bit later on I was not sure where the track went, but fortunately spotted a beater holding a red flag who pointed me in the right direction to Slaggyford, though he suggested I went with him back down to the road. He told me there had been good shooting for the last three days— the land was let out to a syndicate. On the road we parted company and I soon rejoined the Way. My next encounter was of an altogether different kind. Going through a field of inquisitive heifers, I heard strange gruntings from behind a wall and then saw a bull, a huge brown beast with bulging muscles. Fortunately he stayed still as I opened a gate and strode towards the farm. I breathed a sigh of relief when I got there. Presently I was walking by the South Tyne river which would have been pretty but for the weather, and thence to Slaggyford.

The campsite lady was friendly and talkative. Snippets of information included: "There don't seem to be so many caravans these days." "Business is unpredictable." "A party of 12 French walkers came in out of the blue." "Not so much pre-booking." She'd been here for 12 years, but still couldn't get used to the midges.

### Sunday, 24th August

In the morning she chatted to me again, telling me about one young man doing the End to End walk who had recently stayed at the campsite. He was a science teacher, and was raising money for Cancer Research, for cancer ran in his family, though he'd been cleared. Over a cup of coffee with her husband, I heard a story about a South African chap who arrived on a horse having ridden 800 miles from Scotland. I finally left after noon!

It was easy walking and just over an hour later found me in a disappointing pub near Burnstones. The afternoon's walk led along Maiden Way, a continuation of the Roman road, through heather vibrant with bees and the smell of honey. The low clouds of the morning were lifting. The route undulated across the A689 and in due course approached the hum of the A69 at Greenhead, the stepping stone to Hadrian's Wall. I was faced with the choice of turning left to camp, or right to the Greenhead Hotel. I decided on the latter. My arrival coincided with a mini-bus full of drunken women. "Come in for a drink, darling" said one of them.

I was saved by the presence of George and David having supper in the large lounge bar and we compared notes. They then went off with a friend and I was joined by a bearded man who introduced himself as Mike, and who turned out to be on his seventh walk of the Way. "I suppose it's because of the challenge," he said. He had done 20 miles that day and was to be up at 6 a.m. "It's the best time for walking."

The hen party had moved into a back room. Apparently two male strippers were coming but first a female stripper, a good-looking blonde, arrived. As it was beginning to get dark, I walked the quarter mile to the campsite. As I was pitching the tent, a man from one of the static caravans asked "Would you like tea or coffee?" I said coffee and he came back with a steaming mug full. "You are more than welcome," he said. A nice, natural gesture.

### Monday, 25th August

Campsites are nearly always noisy and this was no different with noise from the traffic on the A69 and a few late revellers returning from the pub. Leaving the village I took a wrong turn by some terraced houses, and a woman hanging out her washing remarked: "You're going the wrong way, petal."

Today would be a day for Roman history. A military way followed Hadrian's Wall to supply the garrisons, while another large ditch, the Vallum, marks the extent of the military zone southwards. I met the wall at Walltown Crags turret 45a and walked westwards along the wall itself. Now only some three to four feet high, it originally stood 16ft high, was 6-10ft thick and was serviced by 10,000 troops. It took eight years to complete. There were 12 forts together with many intervening turrets and milecastles. Having reached Walltown Quarry, I retraced my steps and then headed eastwards to Aesica Roman fort, or Great Chesters, where I saw George and David again. They told me that last night they had been taken to a pub in Gilsland which had 200 whiskies, their favourite tipple.

From Chesters I continued east, watching sheep being rounded up at a farm below. "You stupid damned bitch," I heard a man cry as the sheep ran back into the field. It was now a beautiful, sunny after-noon after a hesitant, grey morning; you could see for miles all around. At Steel Rig I could see, to the south, the YHA and the Twice Brewed Inn, but decided to press on as it would mean less walking on the morrow and the weather was so great. Beyond Milecastle 39

I passed climbers equipped with ropes and toggles. Beyond Hotbank Crags I put up the tent, I couldn't resist camping by the wall. There were magnificent views all round on a beautiful evening. Apart from a few stragglers most of the visitors had gone. Later I had it to myself, and enjoyed being on my own.

### Tuesday, 26th August

It was cold during the night and I had a fitful sleep—though not disturbed by any Roman ghosts that are believed to haunt the wall. I must admit I had been a little apprehensive. I left Hadrian's Wall at Rapishaw Gap and headed north once more—to Scotland; unbelievable. I could just make out Housesteads fort to the east and further round Sewingshields Crags, where legend has it King Arthur and his knights are sleeping. The path approached Wark Forest and then plunged into it, with a lovely smell of pine from stacks of logs. The plentiful flies were not so lovely.

Further on I passed George and David taking a break, then pressed on for a meal at Horneystead B & B, which further back had been advertising itself as offering meals. I was tempted by its menu—but what a let down! There was a sign saying 'Closed but help yourself in PW room.' I shouted at the farmhouse's front-door and a little old lady, bent, shuffling with a stick, came out and said her daughter was away; the place wasn't always manned. She showed me into the tack room in which was squeezed a rickety table and assorted chairs. She brought me out some bread, paté, cheese and biscuits, so in the end I had a reasonable meal. I was joined by George and David who after a quick drink left before me. George talked about a new play by Tom Stoppard, author of *Rosencrantz and Guildenstern*, which I had just read. As I left, the old lady gave me an apple. "I feel bad there's not more for you to eat. It wasn't like this in the old days. There was always someone here then."

After walking on a grass track through mellow countryside, there was a steep climb to a radio mast, reached at last. But about an hour later I was in Bellingham stocking up on supplies, before selecting one of the two available campsites. In the Rose and Crown I once more stumbled into George and David. We chatted about *Arcadia*, Tom Stoppard's latest play, then the Astronomer Royal's latest book, based on the concept of there being other universes connected to Black Holes.

*Wednesday, 27th August*

For much of the day I trailed another walker which, at least on the open moorland that confronted me at the start of the day, made for easier navigation. The day was dark, and it rained from time to time. In the early afternoon there was a long slog up to Whitley Pike. I took a late lunch break having at last reached the edge of Kielder Forest, Britain's largest. The weather began to brighten, but it felt good to come off the moors, even if the flies abounded once more. The path initially led round the edge of the forest, then into its depths. In the midst of a plantation planted in 1941 it was very quiet, eerie. Later the path left the forest and followed the River Rede. I passed two farms with the wonderful names of Blackhopeburnhaugh and Cottonshopeburnfoot.

Reaching a campsite by the river, I decided to stop comparatively early. Two young German men arrived in an old Mercedes Benz and set up camp, as did a Swedish couple who had been touring Scotland for three weeks. In mid-evening I wandered along the river to the Byrness Hotel, half a mile away, where I once more found George and David, together with the walker I'd followed that morning, and three other Pennine Way men. George and David gave me their addresses and asked me to send them a card when I either got to John O'Groats, or quit. As we nattered we were joined by the two Germans, one 6ft, the other 6ft 4ins at least, who came in with soaking feet. In the dark they hadn't seen the bridge across an intervening stream and had waded across the ford. We couldn't help laughing. They started asking lots of questions, mainly about beer, whisky and tipping. They avoided a return soaking by having a lift back to the campsite, as did I. It felt odd to be in a car.

*Thursday, 28th August*

There was a frost on the grass and I also noticed that the two Germans were quiet, possibly hung-over. After a steep climb through woodland I arrived at the top of Byrness Hill, with a wonderful view of Redesdale Forest behind me. The route kept to the hillside across a desolate moor, though alongside a fence. Very, very remote. The path ascended to Ravens Knowe, using duckboards to cross a boggy area. Thinking about reaching the Scottish border, I slipped on mud. The border itself was to prove as slippery. After a long slog over boggy moor, I stopped for lunch at Chew Green, site of a Roman camp and which I thought was in Scotland. At last. I'd now walked the entire length of England in nine weeks and two days. It felt good.

Twenty minutes later I definitely believed I'd reached Scotland, having crossed a gate and the border. The route now followed Dere Street, a Roman road, which runs south to York. But I still worried about the border. Although remote, I met two lady walkers on a day trip to Chew Green. One, with grey-hair, commented: "You should be sponsored, you'd raise thousands." I rested at Yearning Saddle shelter where the Way leaves Dere Street. It has bench seats, is clean and tidy, with maps on one wall, a visitors book, and notices about shitting and using a shovel. I left to find I now appeared to be following fences along the border. The route led over Beefstand Hill, with views across to Scotland, mists, and the whaleback shape of The Cheviot, then Mozie Law and Windy Gyle. The latter is magical. At 6.15 p.m. I crossed the fence, and surely I was now in Scotland—it took its time! Slightly further on I decided to pitch camp in a slight dip used by sheep. Even so, it was windy and I had difficulty in putting up the tent. Once up, I went outside and nearly froze to death.

*Friday, 29th August*

It was an uncomfortable, cold night. I'd put on all my clothes, even the anorak hood and gloves. The wind also made it very noisy. I was almost caught in the act by three early walkers. Shortly after leaving I was back in England, walking along flagstones by the border fence. After about an hour I came to a mock grave in the bog by the side of the track marked by a pair of old boots and a makeshift wooden cross. Strangely, further on was a plaque: 'In memory of Stan Hudson, died 12 July, 1981.'

The morning's rain had eased off, but it was now misty and I couldn't see a thing. Climbing up to the top of Cairn Hill, a side path leads to Cheviot Summit, but there was no point in making the excursion in this weather. Further on a quagmire of peat is crossed by a boardwalk to help prevent erosion. In the mist it was easier to become confused, and close up navigation often depended upon following others' boot prints. Once the mist lifted I could see a shelter similar to that at Yearning Saddle, and I used it for my lunch stop. People had left all sorts of dried food packets—soup, oats, coffee, etc. I looked at the visitor's book and was cheered by a couple of entries: 28 August - 'Well, the last day has finally arrived. I'll be glad to be going home but what a hoot, what a walk! (Hello Tony, if you do pass this way - hope you make it to John O'Groats). - Steve, Burtonwood, Cheshire.' Two days' earlier: 'Hi to everyone I've met - it's been brilliant. Next stop John O'Groats. Nicky.' I then spotted George and David heading towards the hut. They had stayed in a guesthouse off the route last night. They had had stiff drinks before supper, with the owner making encouraging comments such as: "A good man doesn't stop drinking." They had sung a few bars of 'Scotland the Brave' on crossing the border.

I left them eating their lunch and reached the Schil after a sharp climb. It provided lovely views down the College Valley of rolling hills with rocky tors in the foreground standing sentinel. Shortly afterwards I crossed into Scotland once more and left England for the last time. The last hill on the Pennine Way is Whitelaw, and the descent into Kirk Yetholm began. The land looked different, with trees and fields, all in all more mellow and quite unlike the remote wilderness of the Cheviots. George and David gradually caught up and we walked into Kirk Yetholm together. At the Border Hotel a big sign says 'End of the Pennine Way', but we were not allowed a free half pint, however, as we didn't have a copy of Wainwright's book. George's wife Grace had arranged to meet the two of them here, and she soon appeared to pick them up and head off to Whitby for a holiday.

A lovely hot bath in a B & B relaxed me, and I felt relieved to have finished the Pennine Way and reached Scotland. 736 miles under the belt. But on the map Scotland looked more difficult than I thought.

# 7. **Scottish Lowlands**

*Saturday, 30th August*

The landlord advised me to take the St Cuthberts way to Jedburgh, but I decided against it because it seemed to go too far south. After trying to find a path over Venchen Hill, I retraced my steps and took the B6352 to Kelso, seven miles away, instead. It was good walking weather—cool but sunny, and the road led through pleasant agricultural land with fields of corn and vegetables and some with livestock.

I arrived in Kelso, described as 'Britain in Bloom Winner', at lunchtime. I could make out the stately Floors Castle and was soon crossing Kelso Bridge, built by John Rennie in 1803 to a design he also used for the larger Waterloo Bridge in London, commenced nine years later. When this Waterloo Bridge was demolished in 1934-36, two of its iron lamp standards were saved and re-erected on Kelso Bridge. In the afternoon I walked round the ruins of the abbey founded by King David in 1128 and destroyed by the Earl of Hertford in 1545. It was built to an unusual double cross plan with two sets of transepts as well as two towers. Having booked into a nearby campsite, courtesy of the TIC, I visited the Red Lion which was open all day. It specialised in real ale with four on cask, most notably Farne Island pale ale. I then stocked up with supplies (including a Selkirk Bannock and a Traquair spice cake), as well as foot care ointments and pads, and for once a bottle of wine.

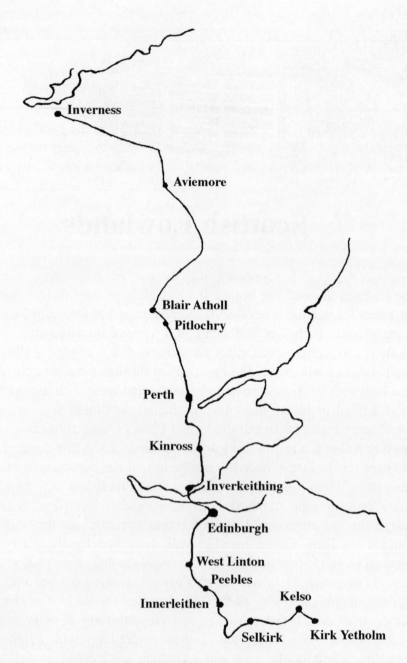

*Through the Scottish Lowlands and Highlands*

When it was found out at the campsite that I was walking to John O'Groats, I was given a can of Tennents special ale as a gift, along with a pint of long life milk! The beer and wine went down pleasantly—it was a celebration of a kind.

### Sunday, 31st August

I woke to the sound of birds playing in the trees at the back of the tent. In the wash-house I passed the cleaning lady mopping the floor as I went to a cubicle. Another man came in who she knew. "Heard the news? Princess Diana was killed at 4 o'clock this morning."

"What" we both exclaimed, "Princess Diana dead!"

The camp owner was almost in tears and the news infected the day; it was difficult to believe, she had so much to live for. During the day my mind played over several questions—what would happen to the two princes; how would the royal family react; would there be a state funeral; how would the nation react.

It was raining as I left and walked by the broad but shallow looking River Teviott to the ruins of Roxburgh Castle on its hillock. I climbed up a steep path through wet grass, but there was nothing much to see of this once royal residence. It was here that James II of Scotland was killed in 1460 when a cannon exploded during his siege of the castle which was then held by the English. Within days his infant son was crowned in Kelso Abbey. Roxburgh village was some distance further on, and I kept to lanes on leaving the place. Fortunately they were very quiet, with hardly any cars. But once in Maxton I had to travel along the A699 to St Boswells. In the Buccleuch Hotel I had a pint of Greenmantle, a local beer from Broughton near Bigar. The conversation in the bar was, perhaps inevitably, about Diana, and quite tearful. However, one customer managed a different subject and told me I could have walked along St Cuthbert's Way to Melrose, the signs for which I saw in Maxton.

For a change I decided to have high tea before heading for Melrose. The route was not that pleasant, with main roads and a by-pass. I passed a middle-aged hitch-hiker on the other side of the road and we had a conversation in between cars. "Be careful; very dangerous road; good youth hostel." As we parted a bus was heading his way. "A bus," I heard him shout gleefully. I went into the Youth Hostel at Melrose, but as no-one was around, I decided against staying. I walked past the abbey ruins and asked a couple if this was the centre of the town. They said they were foreigners who had just come from a campsite that turned out to be 200 yards down the road.

The Ship Inn had no real ale, and after one pint of John Smith's bitter that lacked both the taste and punch of cask, and was too cold, I tried the Kings Arms Hotel, with its sign 'Welcomes walkers'. There I found Farne Island again.

### Monday, 1st September

Today would largely be a touristy day, with Selkirk the destination. It was a damp day, and highly suited to spending more time indoors than usual. Melrose Abbey was founded by David 1 in 1136 and destroyed in 1545. It appears it was Robert the Bruce's last wish that his heart should be taken on Crusade before burial at Melrose, while his body remained with other Scottish kings at Dunfermline. Then I went to see the Trimontium exhibition on Agricola's Three Peaks Roman fort and annexes at Newstead (80-185 A.D.) in the Tweed Valley, including their signal station at Trimontium (the three hills). There was a picture of a Roman tent of leather not much different in style from today's traditional canvas type.

From Melrose I walked along lanes and the banks of the river Tweed to Abbotsford, Sir Walter Scott's mansion. As it was now pouring with rain I first went to the tea-room to dry out. The house itself has the study, still with his desk and chair, where Scott wrote his later novels to pay off his debts. In the corner is a sinister looking cast of Sir Walter Scott's head made after his death. A private stair-case leads from a book-lined gallery up to his bedroom. Scott died in the dining room, his bed having been placed near the window so that he might see his beloved Tweed. The library, a beautiful room with a lovely ceiling, contains row upon row of leather bound books. Abbotsford was one of the first private houses to be lit by gas (in 1824), the gas being made on the premises.

In the shop I bought Hamish Brown's *Pennines to Highlands*, which might provide an alternative route via the Union Canal to the West Highland Way.

The way to Selkirk initially led along a narrow, winding road through woods, then emerged onto the A7. On the edge of the town I passed a camping sign, and took a long walk through an industrial estate and past disused tweed mills to a site that turned out to be next to a swimming pool by a rugby pitch and the river. Great. "We usually charge £7.50, but as there's just youse, you can stay free." What a generous spirit!

Having dined in my tent, I climbed up to the town centre. There's the obligatory statue to Walter Scott with a quotation from *Waverley* in the town square: 'By Yarrows stream still let me stray / Though none should guide my feeble way / Still feel the breeze down Ethrick break/ Although it chill my withered cheek.' Real ale was more difficult to find, but eventually I tracked down The Cross Keys, which served cask Caledonian, and also had the CAMRA newspaper *What's Brewing*. So I improved my knowledge on several more beers.

### Tuesday, 2nd September

I went back into town to take some photos and to shop, and found the impressive monument to Mungo Park, the African explorer and doctor born at Foulshiels, Selkirkshire in 1771 that I'd missed the previous evening. I was also impressed with the Clapperton statue outside Victoria Halls of a soldier, the only survivor of 80 men sent from Selkirk to the Battle of Flodden Field, bearing a blood-stained English flag, erected in 1913 to commemorate the battle's 400th anniversary. I also looked round Scott's courtroom (he had been sheriff of Selkirkshire from 1799 until his death in 1832) which now also served as the town hall. It transpired that Mungo Park was a friend of Scott and, like Scott, was one of 13 children. And I couldn't resist buying another Selkirk bannock from the actual Selkirk Bannock Shop, and a yum-yum!

As the early sunshine changed to clouds and wind, threatening rain, I walked along the A7 alongside Ettrick Water, and through woods to Moffat. At Foulshiels were the remains of the stone house where Mungo Park had been born.

I then took the Minchmoor Trail, turning off the A708 at Yarrowford, as this would form a direct link to the Southern Upland Way, the most sensible way of completing the next stages of the route to John O'Groats. My rucksack seemed heavier for some reason, and I made a note to lighten it again. The Trail led through heathered hills with no-one around. The afternoon was windy, with drizzle in the air. In a forest I came across a log-wood bothy recently built by Forest Enterprise with a sign that stated: 'Walkers Welcome Here'. Made of unsawn logs, still with their bark, it had a verandah in front. Inside were bunk beds made of hardboard, and a table and log chairs. On the road into Traquair I was offered a lift. "I admire a man of principle but I pity your poor feet," the driver said when I declined. After he had explained how I had passed through an area covered in Scottish blood, he exhorted me to "Spit twice on the statue of the Duke of Sutherland, [apparently the culprit], north of Inverness."

I gave Traquair House a miss, and carried on instead to Innerleithen. After some pints of Tennents, I booked into the Tweedside Caravan Park by the river. As I felt I needed cheering up, I had a good meal in a restaurant accompanied by real ale from the Belhaven brewery.

### Wednesday, 3rd September

I still felt dull and listless this morning, so started the day by visiting Robert Smail's printing works, a working museum founded in 1867 which is like stepping back in time. It was taken over by the National Trust for Scotland in 1986 on the retirement of Cowan Smail. Nothing seemed to have changed in the office since 1867, nor with the various printing presses, notably an 1870s Wharfedale Reliance, originally run by a water wheel. It was one of the few printing firms which always composed by hand, the guide explained, never using hot metal.

I still dawdled in the town over lunch, but eventually dragged myself away. I had to retrace my steps to Traquair and past Traquair House, which has its own brewery, but I decided not to go in, before making a seven and a half miles walk along a B road to Peebles. By mid-afternoon I was there and ensconced in the lounge of a B & B near the High Street, having tea out of a delicate china cup with shortbread goodies. But to compound my essential mood, my feet were sore. After stocking up on antiseptic cream, I climbed up to a wooden platform at St Mungo's church to join a bell-ringing session. There were no ropes, just rods and levers to work the 13 bells, which meant that tunes could be played by one person. The middle-aged bell-ringer played 'Rowan Tree', 'Ye Banks and Braes of Bonnie Scotland' and other Scottish songs. "When people celebrate their centenary, and we seem to have quite a number, we play Happy Birthday and their favourite song for them," he said, "or Welsh songs when Wales are playing Scotland at rugby." I had a go and Peebles suffered its worst ever musical experience. In the very broad nave were hanging religious paintings, mostly of Jesus, by Portchmouth Roland, a member of the congregation who later became a minister. The paintings were thought controversial when put up 20 to 30 years ago—I thought they were quite powerful.

After visiting the nearby Bridge Inn and enjoying a couple of pints of Deuchars real ale, I bought two of the three different Traquair bottled beers to take back to the B & B. The label on their Jacobite Ale informed me: 'The famous Bear Gates guarding the approach to Traquair House have been closed since 1745—when the last person to pass through them was Bonnie Prince Charles. Now, 250 years later, the ancient Traquair Brew House celebrates the Jacobite cause by producing this potent spiced ale, to a traditional fine recipe. Sip slowly and remember the old trail to the King o'er the water.' It was treacly, heavy and potent with a hint of chocolate. I liked it.

### Thursday, 4th September

Over breakfast the landlady complained about "those dratted bells. I don't like them, they're not the same as the old ones." I decided to stay another night—my stomach felt a bit upset and I generally needed to recharge my batteries, though I worried about money for I seemed to be spending all the time.

In the council office I joined a queue to sign the Book of Remembrance for Diana, Princess of Wales. Some of the entries in the handsome leather book were very touching: 'Beautiful person, sadly missed', 'We all love you so much', 'I'm so sorry something like this happened to you', 'Goodnight, sweetheart', 'A jewel in the crown', 'A new light shines in heaven', 'Nothing like this should have happened to you.' Amongst those signing the book were many children.

As the Peebles Arts Festival was on, I decided to see 'Flavours of the Scottish Borders' with freelance chef Jane Lauder. I watched her prepare 'Supreme of Tweed Salmon' poached with tarragon and lemon cream sauce, which we were then allowed to taste. Excellent. There was also shortbread and cheese. In the interval before the next dish I went to the Green Tree Hotel, recommended for its real ales. Here I sampled a pint of The Ghillie, Broughton brewed, with a sharpish taste, and then Cumberland Ale, Jennings, Cockermouth brewery, smoother and not so sharp. Back at the Festival the afternoon flavours included 'Supreme of Chicken stuffed with Haggis', served with whisky and mustard sauce and glazed apples. Jane Lauder praised haggis. And the verdict—delicious. Jane used to be the chef at the Hydro in Peebles. "I'd rather work with 20 male chefs than another woman," she said.

Diana still seemed to be on everyone's minds, for joining a party of elderly ladies from Wishart at a coffee table, I heard one lady saying she thought the Queen was late in saying something about Diana and that the Union flag should have been lowered earlier. In the mid-afternoon I made a lovely undemanding walk along the Tweed to the 14th century Neidpath Castle, which stands dramatically on a rocky outcrop above the river. Its walls are nearly 11ft thick and there is a rock hewn well and pit prison.

What decadence, for after a hot bath, with bubbles and shampoo, then a pot of tea and biscuits, I went to another Festival event, 'Words Alive', with Margaret Thomson Davis, an historical novelist. She said that to write you need "an obsession to communicate; a love of people, and curiosity." She herself had picked up lots of stories and dialogue (for her novels) from riding on buses in Glasgow. She finished by referring to her father's journals, which were very moving. I asked her if these would ever be published. "No," she replied, "I'm too close to them."

As the talk ended I spoke with a woman who had been cycling in India recently to raise money for LEPRA. I told her about my walk. "It's good to see a few eccentrics left," was her parting shot. A pint of Greenmantle Ale in the Tontine Hotel was followed by watching the TV news at the guesthouse. The landlady guessed "It will be all about Diana again. It's like a Graham revival meeting."

### Friday, 5th September

Still feeling low, but it proved to be a reasonable day's walking, initially through forest to Romannobridge. *En route* I met a shepherd on an old Honda motor bike. He would like to do my trip some day, he said, though not the far north of Scotland—north of Wick was too cold and desolate and should be cut off and floated away.

At West Linton I was directed to a farm where I could camp in a field. The site and I both felt rather alone and solitary. A pint of Theakston's XB and a supper at the Linton Hotel somewhat cheered me. But I needed a torch to find the tent—the days were definitely shortening.

### Saturday, 6th September

Through rain then drizzle I took a footpath to Carlops. Both the church and pub, the Allan Ramsay, were closed, probably because it was the day of Diana's funeral. Walkers and others, however, seemed to be taking advantage of the day, for several were out, including two men with eagles on their wrists. A group of girls, all dressed up in foul weather gear and with rucksacks and rolled tents, were on the Duke of Edinburgh Award scheme. I partook of lunch in a bus shelter on the A702—at least it was dry! A man in a red Fiesta offered me a lift to Edinburgh; it was sorely tempting.

After some indecision, I decided to go over the Pentlands, although they looked a bit daunting. And it rained all afternoon. I crossed the hills between Bore Stane and Scald Law peaks; on the highest point the rain was almost like hail. I decided on a long trek into Balerno, but wished later that I had continued along the tops of the Pentlands into the heart of Edinburgh. Passing the Mallory Arms I popped in for a pint, but it proved to be the worst pub of the trip. There was loud pop music blaring, the decor was a dingy brown, and the customers were all males. Two nasty looking men with glazed eyes were singing to each other over pints of lager.

I picked up the Water of Leith walk, an old railway track, to Slateford and when I saw a suitable site, a small, level, leafy patch under trees and by a stream, I decided to camp although it was a bit gloomy. I was still feeling unhappy and would have liked to linger in Edinburgh, where I had once lived.

# 8. The Highlands

*Sunday, 7th September*

It proved to be not a very pleasant walk to the Forth Road Bridge, as I constantly changed my mind between more direct main roads with all the traffic, and quieter, older roads. At least it was not raining today, though the day was overcast, as was my head, with a dull headache. Eventually I emerged onto the A90 and stopped at the Hopsacks to be told that lunch could only be taken in the dining room; there were no bar snacks. Still, I had a pint of Theakston's brewery conditioned best bitter. I continued along the A90 before turning into South Queensferry on the B924. Here I found large, luscious blackberries on the side of the road, and I helped myself.

In Dalmeny I paused at St Cuthbert's parish kirk. The stained glass in the apse window was a gift from a Polish officer who fought with the Allies in World War II. While stationed in Scotland he fell in love with the church and gave the glass in memory of his mother, who died in Poland. One shows St Thomas of Poland, another the Madonna and Child and Polish eagle, and the third has St Margaret and the city arms of Edinburgh. In the vault are the remains of the 5th Earl of Rosebery who died in 1929 and who was Prime Minister in 1894-5. A man in the church told me that the Rosebery family used to come regularly but they now favour an Episcopalian church in South Queensferry. Referring to my remonstration that churches seemed to be closed these days, he said: "It's the insurance, if the door is open and you are vandalised, it's your fault." It wasn't far now to the bridge, and an exhilarating crossing surrounded by sea and sky saw me to North Queensferry. The only snag was that I tripped over my shoelace, falling flat on my face and grazing my knee. A plaque indicates some of the differences 74 years can make. Whilst the road bridge opened in 1964, took six years to build, using 390 men of whom two died, the railway bridge, opened in 1890, took eight years to build, required 4,600 men of whom 57 were killed.

As I was gazing back at the bridges from the far side, a small, plump woman and a man asked me about buses. She then asked me where I had come from and when I told her she exclaimed: "Oh, I must take a picture of you." She whipped out a camera and the man took a photo of the two of us. "I should put a medal on your chest now." I found a reasonably priced B & B run by a lady from Surrey, but who had now been in Scotland for 30 years. The B & B was almost under the railway bridge, and suffered from the noise both from the trains and the hum from wind passing through the structure. The local inn, the Albert Hotel, was again disappointing—the bar dingy and the customers rather undesirable, but at least the barmaids were attractive.

### Monday, 8th September

I'd been thinking about sponsorship for my walk for several days, and though it was now almost finished, I thought it might still be possible to raise some money. I had in mind Multiple Sclerosis because an old friend of mine, Alan Slater, suffers from it. I decided I'd phone Gill and discuss it with her that evening.

I left North Queensferry on the Fife Coast Path, bordered by blackberries and sloeberries. I soon reached Inverkeithing where I popped into The Haven Coffee Shop enticed by the sign 'We at the Haven believe in God. Not only de we believe in Him—we know Him!' Then it was an unprepossessing walk along the B981 to Kelty. At a lunch break in a field, a herd of cows appeared and wanted to take part, making directly for me. As I stroked one's nose, I wondered why it is that the end is always so revoltingly wet and runny. Kelty proved to be a rather grey, uninviting village, in which I eventually found somewhere to have a cup of tea. The B road was also the way to Kinross, with fields to either side, filled with cattle or combine harvesters.

I found a caravan and camping site at Gaimez Bridge Farm, where no-one was around and the shop was closed. I decided to erect my tent even though it was very noisy, being close to the M9. Two foreign cyclists arrived later and pitched their tent on the other side of the field. This seemed to spark the arrival of the warden who wanted £5. There was no pub or phonebox nearby, so I couldn't phone Gill regarding sponsorship.

### *Tuesday, 9th September*

It was an horrendous night—both freezing cold, with continuous noise from the motorway and with a loud banging noise from behind the tent. I could feel the cold penetrating my bones. But as it was so cold it prevented me lingering and I was away noticeably early for me. That was good, for now I felt I just wanted to complete the walk.

I breakfasted in Kinross and phoned Gill from Milnathort. She said Diana's funeral on TV was very moving. I floated the idea of fundraising for Multiple Sclerosis and she said she would make enquiries, although she thought I had left it too late.

As I walked along quiet lanes, I recalled smells I had encountered along the trail. They included rotting vegetation—sweet in the fields; the similarly sweet, slightly sickly smell of silage in black plastic bags; of pine from forest trees; of sawn wood from a timber mill; of an earthy, even autumnal smell. The rubbish along the roadsides included Irn Bru, Coke and Budweiser cans, cigarette packets, various chocolate wrappers, tape cassettes and reels of tape, and bits of foam. Round the middle of the day I felt as if I was in the middle of nowhere. The terrain was hilly, with lots of sheep and tall wispy plants with black pods shaking in the wind and making a noise. Gradually I could make out a view of the mountains beyond Perth.

In the late afternoon I reached the village of Forteviot with nice-looking terraced almshouses set around a green. But there were no pubs or shops. A plaque states: 'This village was rebuilt by John

Alexander Ist Baron Forteviot of Dupplin in the years 1925-26 and occupies part of the site of the Pictish capital, Fothur-Tabaicht, a royal residence from the VII to XII centuries—Here Kenneth MacAlpin died AD 860.' The wind died completely as I walked on for what seemed like ages, round the Dupplin Castle estate. Just before 7 p.m. I could see Perth, and was soon booked into a campsite on the outskirts of the town, near a pub, the Cherrybank. But the pub had brewery conditioned, not cask, beer though it still tasted good, perhaps because I had walked 22 miles in the day. I even left the pub feeling slightly merry.

### Wednesday, 10th September

Yet another cold, almost frosty, and noisy night—why are campsites so close to main roads! Chatting with the driver of a campervan, I learned of a man in an electric wheelchair who was raising funds whilst going round the coast and staying with fellow CB enthusiasts. Dallied in Perth in the morning, in part to have my boots sealed round their rims, and in part to hunt out a two season sleeping-bag, which I found on reduced offer. I parcelled off the blanket to sister Jenny's.

It was a glorious, sunny day, the first for a while, and it felt good to be on the road in the afternoon, though not on the A9 which I ended up on by my usual mistake. In Luncarty I decided to press on towards Glen Shee along the B8063.

Later I turned down a lift but stood chatting to the driver, who proved to work for Scottish National Heritage, about John Muir, the great Scots outdoors man and conservationist whose works I had read. He believed more people should know about Muir and that there should be a National Park in his honour. I couldn't agree more—he is inspirational.

As evening came on I asked at a farm if I could camp. An elderly man was fetched and said: "I think we will be able to provide at least that for you," pointing to a nice open area in front of the house. As I pitched my tent, a schoolboy came and asked if I would like a cup of tea, promptly returning with a mug and half a packet of biscuits. The new sleeping bag looked odd—it was turquoise and pink, slightly effeminate, whilst the other new item, a dehydrated sweet and sour chicken with rice was quick and easy to make. But it proved tasteless and not very satisfying.

### Thursday, 11th September

I was woken at 7.20 a.m. by the schoolboy. "I've brought you some breakfast. I'm sorry if I've woken you."

I ate honeyed toast and tea in my sleeping bag—which had kept me snug all night. What had I been missing! When I departed, no-one was at home, so I left a note. There were lots of low, dark misty clouds about and it felt as if it would rain—in fact it turned out sunny later. It wasn't long before I was in Glen Shee, a wild and desolate place, with bracken covered hills. As I walked on there was a smell of smoke as if from a bracken fire, and presently I could see the fire itself. A Conservancy Land Rover stopped. "Thought you were going to the fire," I said.

"It'll burn itself out," replied the ranger, a young man with fair, receding hair. "Seen anything interesting?"

"A black rabbit."

"That's good, it's lucky."

The afternoon was spent in finding tracks, losing them as they petered out, wading through thick heather, and stumbling onto another track until that too ran out, or veered the wrong way. At 7.15 p.m., feeling really weary, I stumbled into Aberfeldy passing a polling station—it was the vote on Scottish devolution. I just couldn't resist falling into the Black Watch and quaffing a pint of Dark Island real ale from Orkney. It was light in colour, although the barmaid said it should be darker. But it had a good, strong taste. I enjoyed it so much that I had three pints, and a meal. Considerably revived, I found the conveniently placed Aberfeldy campsite and pitched tent. I was surprised to find that the nearby Palace Hotel had Waggle Dance. I felt happy—even though it had been an exhausting day's walk, but I had covered some 20 miles. I was making excellent progress.

### Friday, 12th September

Perhaps unsurprisingly, I felt hungover next morning. Newspaper headlines recalled 'Yes - Scotland voted Yes and Yes'. In the Tourist Office an elderly male assistant told me he wasn't sure devolution was a good thing. 'I've always had my reservations, but it's done now.'

The day's route began along a minor road along the River Tay, on a day that was blessed with, or suffered from the whole range of weather—sun, rain and hail. Then I found a Scottish Rights of Way Society footpath over gentle hills to Pitlochry. Looking back I could see smoke from another fire near Aberfeldy. On the edge of Pitlochry I passed the Festival Theatre; 'Mrs. Warren's Profession' by Bernard Shaw was on and I considered going that evening. I bypassed the dam and fish ladder by the theatre, as I had seen them on a previous visit.

I booked into the Milton of Fonab caravan site having queried the price. The lady at reception responded simply by asking, "Do you want it or not." It was in fact a good site in all respects. Another woman at reception subsequently told me of a pub in Moulin Square, a mile away, specialising in real ale with its own brewery. Bernard Shaw was off. The Moulin Inn turned out to have been established in 1695 and its brewery was the only one in Perthshire and one of Scotland's smallest.

I tried Braveheart—a 'light, golden, smooth bitter', then Ale of Atholl—a 'slightly sweet, malty, stronger ale'. I preferred the latter, but then went for Old Remedial—'full-bodied, rich, strong', that reminded me of Old Peculier, though not so dark nor so thick, but as strong. The inn was very busy and there was a guy singing and playing a guitar in an adjoining room. I fell into conversation with a tall, rangy man, with greyish hair and a white moustache who, it turned out, lived down the road from me in Worcester. Ian had just finished a four week holiday in the mountains, seeing the wilderness. He didn't find many pubs in Scotland selling real ale, but enjoyed this one leaving, like me, a little the worse for wear. I had had six pints. So much for my vow all those miles back.

*Saturday, 13th September*

Sure enough, I had a hangover. So perhaps it was best to go for the hair of the dog and start the day by visiting the Blair Athol Distillery. According to a short film, there used to be 93 distilleries in the Central Highlands, now there are only five. The fermented liquid, called the wash, is distilled twice, and the resultant mush or pot ale syrup is fed to sheep in winter mix as a treat. The copper stills look like huge gourds. The water used comes from the Benbrashie burn. "It's tasted every day," said the guide, Jackie "and nothing is taken out except the odd salmon."

It's left to age in Spanish sherry oak casks for three years, or eight if it is to make special malt. Whilst tasting several whiskies at the end of the tour, I chatted to a party of four English holidaymakers who had been to the Martell distillery in France. One mentioned that Jackie had talked of a 2% loss through evaporation every year when the whisky is in cask. "In France, they call this the Angels' share."

I set off in time to visit the Pitlochry Highland Games, the first such games I'd ever visited and the last to be held in Scotland that year. Chatting to a member of the countryside ranger service, he felt that the Scottish referendum would further the cause of more access to the countryside as there would be no interference from the House of Lords.

I watched the 16lb hammer throwing competition, the hammer being described in the programme notes as a blacksmith's heavy sledgehammer with a long wooden shaft. No turning is allowed. Bruce Aitkin, a young giant, broke the ground and British record by more than a metre with a huge throw of 153ft. Then came the 22lb hammer event: the first hammer, or rather the shaft, broke, and a new one was called for. Bruce Aitkin was the winner again, but without setting a record. A Tug-of-War competition also raged. Whilst watching the 28lb weight hammer throwing, Ian from Worcester turned up. "Are you malingering?" he joked. Together we watched Tossing the Caber, the winner being the one who tosses the caber the straightest—"a perfect throw is one which goes straight over, with the light end landing at 12 o'clock precisely," as the announcer informed us.

Half an hour after leaving the games I'd reached the Boat House café by Loch Fascally, remembered from a previous visit and had a very nostalgic tea. On through Fascally Woods and under the Tummel bridge I arrived at the now closed Killiecrankie Visitors' Centre.

Close to 7 p.m. I passed 'Soldier's Leap', a large flat rock at the water's edge from which Donald MacBean, a redcoat soldier fleeing the disastrous battle of Killiecrankie, leapt 18ft across the River Gary while being pursued by Jacobite clansmen. It's odd how many battles between the English and the Scots seem to have been 'disastrous' for one side or the other. Nearby I met a couple walking a dog. They had just driven up that morning from Newcastle for a holiday—it reminded me that it didn't take long by car! Walking along the lane by Gary to Blair Atholl I disturbed a deer in the gathering dusk. At the Atholl Arms Hotel, a large impressive hotel with a grand looking dining room, I went into the public bar—I knew my place! After some Guinness, as there was no real ale, I booked into the nearby campsite and pitched the tent in darkness.

### Sunday, 14th September

The night was disturbed by three revellers, young lads, "f— this", "f— that", laughing, closing and opening car doors umpteen times. The ducks, also disturbed by the noise, added to the cacophony. The night was cold and I needed the anorak over me despite the new sleeping-bag. The year was advancing.

I phoned Gill from the campsite. She had contacted the Multiple Sclerosis Society's headquarters, who told her they had a pack to give to sponsors before the event. The girl at the end of the phone didn't know what else she could do.

I was soon at Blair Atholl Castle which I decided to visit. This is an impressive white building with roof-top turrets. Bonnie Prince Charlie stayed there as did Queen Victoria and Albert (once for three weeks). A sign on a needle-work fire-screen in the small drawing room noted that these were much in demand in the 18th century when ladies used make-up that contained wax. "The screens kept the fire off their faces and so prevented the wax melting so they remained pale and interesting." There was plenty more to see, including marvellous sets of China; geometric patterns of guns, swords and shields in the armoury; and hundreds of antlers on the walls of the ballroom. I left the castle along the Hercules Path through the estate and into woods along a country lane by the River Tilt. A couple of hours out I saw a middle-aged woman walker walking towards me. "Hello again," she said. It was a woman I'd met several days previously when coming across Glen Shee. "Your pack is unmistakable! Who knows, we might meet again."

A tractor, buggy, two Land Rovers and occasional cottage rather spoilt the remoteness of Glen Tilt, but soon I was in an amazing long valley with steep sloping hills either side, green for the most part with little white dots—sheep—high up. A heavy shower came on and once it cleared I decided to camp. It soon started raining again, indeed it rained all evening.

### *Monday, 15th September*

Lashing rain and wind battered my tent all night. A bit eerie. It was still raining when I was fully awake. I felt a slight trepidation at the thought of having to traverse the Cairngorm Mountains with the nearest civilisation at Aviemore. At least the sun came out as I left and I soon came to an old suspension bridge, made of wire and wood, at the Falls of Tarf. This bridge was erected in 1886 to commemorate the death of Francis John Bedford, aged 18, who drowned near here. Brown, white flecked water snarled underneath. But it was an only bridge and I was soon fording lots of small streams, before coming to a big one, swollen by the recent rain. I went up and down several times before I plumped on the best spot to cross, and made it with my feet still dry. The track seemed to go on and on, and I wondered when I was going to get to White Bridge and the turning to Glen Dee. I also saw more streams without bridges marked on the map.

I took a lunch break by the ruins of an old cottage where Queen Victoria had tea during a visit in 1861. It was still very windy. Soon after leaving I came to another stream—Bynack Burn. I took off my boots and socks and tried to wade across but knew I couldn't do it, for the water was too cold and the rocks too sharp

111

and slippery. I just had to cross with them on. Then I came to what I thought was the last stream to cross, and waded across, the sun glinting on the swirling water. I took my boots off, dried my feet and squeezed the water out of my socks. But alas, there was another one—Geldie Burn—wide and forbidding, and fast-flowing. There was nothing for it but to plunge in and the water came over my knees, up to my thighs. At one point I worried about losing my footing and being swept downstream. My boots and socks were now completely soaked, and the wind seemed even colder, but through a forest plantation I at last reached White Bridge over the river Dee. Once over I took the track up Glen Dee leading to the famous Lairig Ghru pass. The ground became very boggy underfoot, and the scenery awesome as I approached Devil's Point, whilst the wind screeched down Glen Geusachan and nearly knocked me over.

There was mist ahead as I came to Ben MacDui, Britain's second highest peak on my right, and ahead to the left Cairn Toul and Braeriach, the third and fourth highest. Lairig Ghru lived up to its name of gloomy or forbidding. I started to really struggle in the gale-force wind. As evening came on I saw three tents, and two men with what looked like fishing rods. That at least was heartening. I thought about camping nearby, but continued on, soon crossing a field of boulders around a lake. As the light started to fade I spotted a place to pitch the tent, but it was easier said than done. A gust of wind blew my groundsheet into a pool, whilst the tent kept ballooning up and it wouldn't stay in place, the tent pegs not holding in the soft, tufty grass. I decided to abandon putting up the tent, and adopted survival tactics, using the survival bag and sleeping bag. In fact, it was lovely to see the stars and later the moon and clouds go speeding overhead. But the air was bitterly cold and I tried to keep my face generally covered. I slept reasonably well, considering.

*Tuesday, 16th September*

I was up early with the light, and after trying unsuccessfully to find five missing tent pegs, I went on my way. Fortunately the night had been rain free, but now it came on. The path was full of boulders and puddles and was easy to lose—indeed at one point I was about to ascend one of the peaks before I realised my mistake. Eventually I reached the forest area and embraced the first tree I came to, a silver birch. My spirits rose, though I soon found the walking nearly as difficult as through Lairig Ghru, for the tree roots made the ground bumpy and uneven.

I soon met two walkers. "Are you all right? It must have been blowy out there," they asked, with some concern. One, middle-aged, said his tent at the campsite below was blown about by wind and his poles broke. I trudged on through pine trees, feeling weary and constantly aware that my hands had become numb, and that my feet were sodden—I might as well have been wading through a stream all day. The path gradually became easier and I eventually came to Coylumbridge where the campsite was closed. But I wasn't intending staying; I took the road to Aviemore.

I stumbled into the Rothiemurchas Visitors' Centre café in Inverdruie, dripping with water and sank down onto a chair. I piled in hot food and drink, there was also an open fire. Thankfully and gradually, my body began to feel better. I left a pool of water where I'd been sitting. At Aviemore Tourist Information Office, I booked into a B & B.

Aviemore High Street is dominated by restaurants, food shops and camping/skiing shops—all useful for my purposes, the latter to stock up on tent pegs. The assistant recommended the Winking Owl for real ale, and I was soon sampling a pint of Orkney Dark Island, a dark, good tasting, strong pint that went down well.

Later on I tried the Old Bridge Inn, this one recommended by my landlady. Old Bridge Inn Heavy was a full-bodied premium cask ale—good, dark, and very nice, and Tomintoul Wild Cat brewed in Scotland's highest brewery. I enjoyed a Highland meal of haggis, neeps 'n' tatties, followed by poached salmon with baked potatoes and salad, and an Eckle-feekin sweet (or walnuts and fruit). Two musicians, a man on guitar and a girl on a flute, started to play folky/bluey music, as they described it, but I gained the feeling that most of the clientele, including some Americans, wanted them to sing Scottish songs. I left feeling full and satisfied.

Back in the B & B lounge, en route for the 10 o'clock news on my room's TV, I met Alison, a 46 year-old freelance journalist working for the *Sunday Times* amongst others, and George, who asked me about my walk. "Did you come through the Lairig Ghru? I'm asking you these questions now because I'm never in a good mood at breakfast." Alison decided she wanted to interview me, but then spent most of the time talking about herself. I didn't go to bed till 12.30 a.m. She also smoked a lot. Journalists!

# 9. **The Last Stages**

*Wednesday, 17th September*

At breakfast, George, who turned out to be a retired university lecturer from Dublin, decided to talk. He also turned out to be keen on walking, had done a number of Munros (Scottish peaks over 3,000 ft) and blamed Hamish MacInnes for starting the craze. He also muttered that women skimmed through books and never knew what was in the middle, nor did he like Botham until he found out he was reading a book he liked. He then confirmed that he wouldn't be in a good mood until he'd had his coffee at 11 a.m. Alison then asked for five minutes for an interview which went on for over an hour. She said she might do a piece for 'a day in the life of' for *The Sunday Times* colour supplement. She still talked and smoked an awful lot.

Having stocked up on supplies, I then bumped into Alison in the Coffee House. She appointed herself my publicist—I don't know whether she meant it—and said she would arrange for a photographer to meet me at the Eastgate Backpackers Hostel in Inverness.

I eventually left Aviemore at 1.30 p.m. I had enjoyed my stay, although a lot of people run the place down. I walked along the road to Carrbridge before turning onto General Wade's road towards Slochd. The weather was just right for walking. Once over Wade's bridge at Sluggan, I saw a possible clearing amongst trees off the track and as the weather was beginning to deteriorate, I decided to set up camp.

115

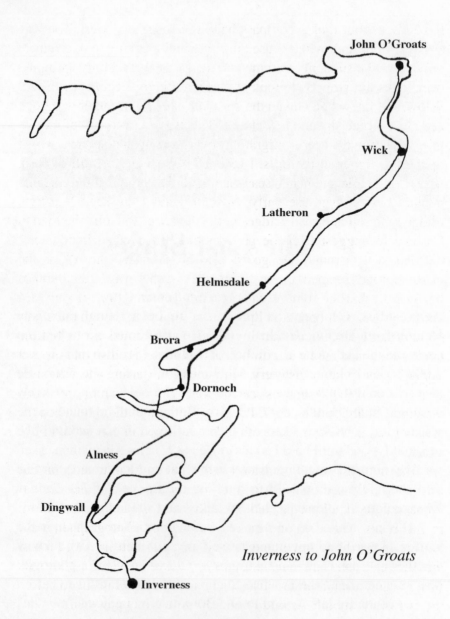

*Inverness to John O'Groats*

## Thursday, 18th September

I slept fitfully for almost 12 hours, and woke feeling cold. There was a frost. During the night there had also been the sounds of an animal, probably a deer, in agony or forlorn and also the bark of a dog which echoed. One vehicle went by. I was soon faced with the choice of three tracks, but took a compass bearing and headed west. The way crossed moorland, with grouse quacking and clucking, also a female red deer—she suddenly saw me and turned tail, gracefully springing over rocks but stopped to look at me. Eventually I could see the A9 below, so I knew I had taken the correct route. The weather was good and clear—blue sky and few clouds. The morning was full of incredible bird noise—geese migrating overhead made sounds which seemed to linger in the hills. I reached a wooden hut, full of flies, with a long table and bench seats taking all the room. I could imagine hunters having a grouse party. Near Tomatin I crossed a concrete bridge with rail and road bridges in the distance, and took the road to Garbole as suggested in the guide-book. But over an hour later I decided to turn round and go back to Tomatin and the A9, as the Garbole road seemed to be going the wrong way. Ten minutes beyond my earlier route I came to the Tomatin Inn—if only I'd known. It was still open and I popped in for a pint, though there was no real ale. I discovered that Inverness was 15 miles away, but the landlord advised me I was now on the best route. He also told me that Tomatin has its own distillery, with a large number of warehouses containing 120,000 barrels of whisky. I soon came upon this distillery, established in 1897. I was looking round the shop when the assistant said: "Now that the others have all gone I can let you have a taste."

Further on I saw a roadside Little Chef and had to stop for old time's sake (I used to work for the owners) and had some nice but innocuous food, all pre-packed. I telephoned the Backpackers hostel in Inverness. There was no message from any photographer, but I booked in for the following night. Just as it was getting dark I found the Auchnahillan Caravan and Camping Centre, Daviot East, with its own bar and restaurant. I realised there were just 12 days to go before the end of the month—could I reach John O'Groats by then?

### Friday, 19th September

I had a musical awakening due to lovely long liquid birdsong. The day was a little nippy and damp, but the sun came out nicely. Though starting along the A9 I soon came onto a B road, taking a

117

short cut across a springy suspension bridge over a river. I soon had a view of the Moray Firth, and not long afterwards of Inverness. A mere half hour later I was in Harry Ramsden's gulping down Harry's Special Haddock in traditional batter, followed by St Clementine sweet. Everything was fresh and well cooked. There was even haggis on the menu.

In the town centre I claimed my place at the Eastgate Backpackers Hostel, indeed having single occupation of a twin-room. The warden, a nice friendly guy, said there were no messages—was this photographer going to get in touch? More and more I just wanted to complete the walk—I had felt a slight chest pain yesterday and that morning, also a certain numbness in my right arm—a touch of arthritis perhaps? In addition my stomach was a little upset and I had bad indigestion. I used the town to stock up on supplies, and two Ordnance Survey maps for the next stages. In the evening I visited the Blackfriars enjoying a pint of Culloden, from Tomintoul—a sharp, strong pint that went down well.

I had disappointingly spotted that my favourite Indian restaurant in Scotland after the Kalpna in Edinburgh, was now an Italian pasta restaurant, but set on the idea of an Indian meal I found another. Then it was back to the Blackfriars and Theakston's Old Peculier—brilliant. The pub had a row of nine cask ales, including two Scottish, also bare floors and a helpful barman. The drinkers appeared roughish, including two Japanese female tourists drinking pints.

### Saturday, 20th September

No message from the photographer, so that was that. My right foot, actually one of the toes, had been feeling increasingly sore—and today it was bad. But it being a sunny, cold day, it was a good one to push on. Whilst undertaking repairs to my toe in a little village by Beauly Firth, a bearded man and a girl came up and expressed concern at my limping through their village. "Come and have a coffee," Gordon said. I went to Gordon's house, met his wife, Margaret, a physiotherapist, and enjoyed coffee and carrot cake. They were concerned about my foot and offered advice—weighing my pack they found it was over three stone, more than it weighed at the beginning of the trip. I must lighten it. They offered to look at my foot and bathe it, and advised my wearing plimsolls for a change, so I left with my boots hanging around my neck.

The route led past a loch to Milton, but beyond the village a grass track I followed became a tunnel of nettles. There was no sensible detour, so I put on my over trousers and waded through, eventually reaching a minor road to Drynie. I passed through Newmore and Bishop Kimbell before reaching the A682 to Conon Bridge, and so the Conon Hotel. "What's cask ale?" said the landlady in response to my question, so I was faced with a pint of Caffreys before heading on to Dingwall where I found a pleasant campsite in fading light close to the town.

I drank Antiquary, a 12 year-old miniature, in bed to celebrate the completion of 1,000 miles!

### Sunday, 21st September

I woke to more lovely bird songs and a sore foot. So it would be plimsolls again. I took the old road to Evanton with views over Cromarty Firth. The weather was still overcast, but my foot was standing its task and I pressed on, reaching Alness in mid-afternoon. After finding all the B & Bs had no-one at home, and likewise the reception at the County Hotel, I was eventually guided to the Station Hotel. My guide, a youth, told me "I work off-shore." It transpires he worked on the giant wheel I saw earlier on the Firth, like a giant Mississippi boat. "We roll the pipes together and wrap them round the wheel, all sizes and they're exported all over the world." The Station Hotel looked run down and we entered a seedy bar full of smoke. I was shown a small but adequate, if dirty looking room which I decided to take. "It's for working men mainly," the manager explained. After a hot shower, I saw to my small toe, which was red and swollen. I squeezed out much pus, an operation I carried out again later in the evening.

The lounge bar of the hotel was full of loud music and pin-ball machines, and the beer was McEwan's Export, not very nice and too cold. The conversation at the bar consisted of "f— this" and "f— that". I retired to my room for supper, cooking a meal on the floor.

*Monday, 22nd September*

The night was disturbed with various comings and goings from neighbouring rooms, but my toe seemed better. I swapped from plimsolls to boots and back again during the day to help. I kept to the A9 to keep the going easy, taking the minor roads to Tain and then Dornoch. The clouds were low, and there was often mist. Beyond Tain I visited the Glenmorangie distillery, along with half a dozen members of the Boyce Hill Golf Club, on a tour led by an attractive young lady. The water here is hard, usually it is soft for whiskies, and mineral rich. Their storage casks come from Missouri and they have previously held Kentucky bourbon. The barrels are first burnt inside. Glenmorangie is an independent, family owned business, the girl explained, producing 2.7 million litres in 1996, making it number one in Scotland and third in the world. The work was done by 16 men. She pointed out two special barrels, one marked 'Duke of York - July 14th 1997', although he said he was teetotal, and the other marked 'Rebecca Stephen - May, 1993', after the first British woman to conquer Everest. In the shop I tasted a ten year-old Glenmorangie, being advised to add water, as it helps to release the flavour. Glenmorangie is Gaelic for Glen of Tranquillity, and is the name for the whole bay area. They also had port, madeira and sherry flavoured Glenmorangie which had been finished in casks originally containing those drinks.

I crossed the new bridge over Dornoch Firth, which was indeed very tranquil and beyond was soon onto a side road to Dornoch. Dornoch was a nice quiet town, and I found a campsite on the beach. My evening's drinking started in the Dornoch Inn. "Have you any cask ales?" I enquired.

"No, this is the land of whisky, not beer," said the English barman. "We don't drink much beer here." His partner added: "In England there is no choice of whisky."

Next I visited the Eagle Hotel, where again there was no cask ale. But I started with a pint of McEwan's and a meal, followed by a couple of whiskies—a Glenmorangie, of course, and a Dalmore from the Alness distillery.

*Tuesday, 23rd September*

I was woken by seagulls to find a bright, sunny, warm day. I walked back into Dornoch for breakfast at a baker's-cum-coffee shop, then visited the fairly plain cathedral built by Bishop Gilbert in 1224-1239. The main features were its stained glass and gargoyles on the exterior. Leaving the town I passed a butcher's shop, I.B. Milburn, advertising exotic meats such as kangaroo, crocodile, ostrich, wild boar, goat, quail, pheasant, springbok steaks, and venison sausages. Chatting to the butcher it transpired that the ostrich was local, whilst the crocodile meat came from Louisiana.

I walked along tracks by the sea to Embo which turned out to be twinned with Kaunakakai, Hawaii. Then it was back on the road to Golspie, full of blackberries and dragonflies. Whilst I sat down for my lunch, a weasel went up the side of the road. A bit later it came back, once crossing the lane and rearing up on hind legs to look, then came back to my side, stopping to peer down tracks in the grass, and then unbelievably it came right past me, only feet away. I turned and then it realised something was up and it shot off into the verge. It had a lovely white chest. The sun was now very warm.

During this day and the next I could hear aircraft and the sound of bombs from the bombing range in the sea off Tain. It was often disquieting and affected my enjoyment of the area.

Past the motionless Loch Fleet it was back onto the A9 which was no fun walking along as I had to keep getting off the road, especially for lorries. I finally reached Golspie and passed the statue on the hill top that I'd been looking at for miles. I spat in its direction in case it was the Duke of Sutherland, as I had promised, not being sure whether I'd done the right thing. In the Stag's Head I enjoyed afternoon tea.

Leaving Golspie there was a Land Rover with a hunting party. "Harris hawks," a woman said. I kept to the sea shore, admiring the sinking sun, the calmness of the sea lapping against rocks, and the call of sea-birds. Soon I was passing Dunrobin Castle, the ancestral home of the earls of Sutherland. I refrained from spitting again. It looks a bit like a fairytale castle with lots of pointed turrets. A small fishing boat, the first vessel I'd seen, was out to sea. It was enchanting walking along that grassy path. Leaves were falling off trees, although there was no wind. Looking back I could still see the statue over Golspie. I passed a 2,000 year-old broch, Carn Liath, but decided not to stop. Though it was only 6.40 p.m., the light was beginning to go. A young boy with two dogs told me I would soon reach a river a bit further on and access back to the A9. In Brora I found a young man sitting on a seat eating a take-away supper who said he was staying at a site about a mile out of town. I plodded on, passing a road sign that said John O'Groats 63.

I finally came to the campsite at Dalchalm, about two miles outside Brora. As I set up tent by the toilets for light, a voice called out: "Are you going to John O'Groats? Go along the A9, its quiet at times and the shortest route. Expect you'll find it an anti-climax. What do you do next?"

*Wednesday, 24th September*

There was a ground frost in the morning, but it promised to be a lovely day again. Walking along the A9 I noticed the details of every mangled seagull, and one stoat. I hoped the three stags' heads outside a shed proclaiming Northern Natural History Taxidermist hadn't been obtained the same way. In one layby a plaque read: 'To mark the place near which (according to Scrope's Art of Deerstalking), the last wolf in Sutherland was killed by the hunter, Polson, in or about the year 1700.' In Lothbeg I could have turned inland for Thurso, but decided to stick to the A9 and the east coast, the quickest route.

Another mental game on this stretch was to guess which brand of lorry or product would be the next. In the early afternoon a Land Rover went by, stopped, the horn blared, and I looked round to see Nicky running towards me. We had a big hug in the road. She got to John O'Groats on 22 September, having travelled via Thurso. She said it had been cold and remote in the mountains, with ice on her tent for two nights. Apparently there were not many walkers in the John O'Groats book this year. "Give me a ring and we'll exchange notes," Nicky said as she got back into the Land Rover and drove off. Unbelievably I had earlier been thinking that I hadn't met anyone I knew.

In mid-afternoon I reached Helmsdale and decided on a B & B for the night, near the harbour. The owner, an elderly lady, showed me an attic room and brought me a teapot and plate of scones. "I always know that cyclists and walkers will be hungry." But she went on to tell me she was let down by one charming cyclist who left without paying. It was beautiful outside and I felt guilty being indoors, but I took a lovely hot bath.

My beer for the night was Miller Pilsner in the Belgrave Arms Hotel. Phoning Gill from the hotel, she said she had phoned the Multiple Sclerosis head office again and spoken to several people; eventually a PR chap said I didn't have to be registered to raise money but it would have to be sent direct to the society. There wasn't much chance of that now!

Three of us each ate alone that evening in the hotel—myself, a Swiss woman, and a young man reading a Peter Mayle book and drinking a double Isle of Jura. We didn't say a word to each other.

*Thursday, 25th September*

I had a slightly troubled night, disturbed by a TV Natural History programme about sharks attacking albatross chicks that I'd watched in the lounge. Another sunny day promised, still and calm. Leaving Helmsdale was a sign that indicated John O'Groats was just 53 miles away.

It proved to be a day of climbing and descending and was hot work. At lunchtime John O'Groats had reduced to 47 miles distant.

I came across a herd of llamas in the afternoon at Kings Park Llama Farm, Berriedale Braes. Apparently the owner started keeping them 10 years previously in Bristol. Now they also keep chipmunks, cockatoos, Vietnamese pigs and others. Lots of school children come to visit. "Do you eat the Llamas?" I innocently asked.

"Good heavens no, they cost £2,000 each and they're pets." Then, changing tack, "Lot of End to Enders go by. Just recently two lots on tandem bicycles, an American and a Dutch couple. One man from Bridgwater does it every year for charity."

The road dropped back to near the sea and I was soon in Dunbeath. Seeing a sign that said: 'Birthplace of Neil Gunn' that pointed to the Heritage Centre, I paid a visit to discover he is 'North Scotland's most famous author' with such titles as *Morning Tide*, *The Silver Darlings*, and *Highland River*. He died in 1973. In the Dunbeath Hotel I enquired about cask ale. "No," replied the landlord. So it was a pint of Tennent's lager. "Get a lot of walkers, two kinds, those doing it leisurely like yourself or those doing it quickly."

On leaving I note a plaque: 'Neil M Gunn, Highland Writer, was born here on 8th November, 1891' above the door of a terraced house next to the Spar shop. There was also a sign which read: John O'Groats 38.

I found the campsite and put up my tent as the weather seemed to change, becoming cold and misty. I then went to the nearby Inver Arms and had a pint of Gillespie's malt stout. The inn had a lovely view and two pleasant girls behind the bar. With their help I also tried some of the local whiskies.

### Friday, 26th September

I woke once more to the sound of birds and an overcast morning. It took an hour to reach Latheron, and more and more people seemed to be aware of the end to end game—a car driver waved, and a lorry driver waved and flashed his lights. In Latheron a church had been converted into a Clan Gunn museum. The village of Lybster turned out to be twinned with Mackinac, USA, due, I discovered, to the life of Lieutenant-General Patrick Sinclair of Lybster who not only founded the harbour here, but who also served in North America between 1759 and 1784 against the French and Indians, and then with the Royal Highland Emigrant Regiment during the American Revolution when he was Lieutenant-Governor of the Port of Michilimackina and founded and commanded Fort Mackinac. Seeing a sign to Caithness Cheese, I fancied a nibble. The owners were out but their young son let me in. His father started the business three or four years ago. They owned nine Freisian, one Jersey and one Angus cow, and sell mainly to shops in Wick and the surrounding area. "I suppose you'll be expanding?" I ask.

"Dad's happy the way it is and definitely not supermarkets," he replied.

As I left the weather had improved with the sun now out. In the afternoon I visited the Kyleburn sweet factory, started 20 years ago by Mackie Donn who thought he could make sweets better than the ones he delivered. The factory now produced 34 different sweets and employed nine people, but Mackie Donn died in April. Among the sweets I noticed Horehound, which is good for colds. I left, sucking horehounds.

On the road to Wick a brown coloured sheep kept walking in front of me, causing traffic problems. There was pain around my hips due to the weight of the pack, and my back and feet were hurting. Passing a B & B in Wick, I couldn't resist the temptation. But beer choice was restricted to Guinness.

### Saturday, 27th September

The forecast was sunny for my last day, but it dawned dull and over-cast—the sun emerging later. In the bakery where I stocked up on supplies, the three ladies wished me well on my last lap. "Expect you'll be getting the train or bus back," one joked.

I felt good. Two cyclists pedalled by, off to Land's End, and I received acknowledgement from some motorists, who waved or tooted. I sang out loud a rendition of 'White Christmas' to some cows. Some sheep wanted to hear it too. By the crematorium in Keis I met a 74 year-old doctor, who did the walk in 1974, setting out on a second attempt. He had an old fashioned rucksack, a stick and a recorder into which he asked me to say a few words. Better than a note-book, he said. He was staying at youth hostels on his journey. I wished him well.

Over the crest of the last hill I could see the island of Stroma. I was savouring these last miles. At the Warth Hill viewpoint, a plaque told me how John O'Groats gained its name from Jan de Grot, a ferryman of Dutch origin who was granted the lands of Wares and Duncansby by the Earl of Caithness in 1489. A legend has it that to deal with his eight disputing sons he built an octagonal table, so that each son could sit at the 'head' of the family. He is buried in Canisbay churchyard. At 5.10 p.m. I crossed the finishing line at the John O'Groats House Hotel—it was something of an anti-climax to say the least. There was no-one around to witness my epic journey of 1,150 miles in 14 weeks and five days. You would have thought there might have been a few tourists at least. I went into the Groats Inn for a celebratory pint of Theakston's best bitter (shame, it was only brewery conditioned). I got the barmaid to take a photo of me crossing the line and outside the hotel front. She turned down the offer of a drink, patting her stomach—she was expecting her third. I signed the large End to End book, and was handed an envelope containing a congratulatory card from my sister Gill and, most welcome, a cheque for £25 to help celebrate.

Over a second pint of Theakston's and a John O'Groats whisky made by Drambuie, I decided to treat myself to an *en suite* room with TV—at precisely £25. I then luxuriated in a very hot bath. I ate alone in the bar, with a bottle of wine to help celebrate, then joined a couple, Dave and Moira, who were just starting their second bottle of wine. "I'll take care of the wine," said Dave, ordering two more bottles and we were all well away.

"I would really like to do this walk sometime," said Moira, a keen walker who used to live in the Lake District. "Dave isn't really keen on walking."

It transpired this was due to Dave having a false leg, as a result of a motorcycling accident in which his best friend was killed. We all became maudlin in our cups.

The long-suffering barman took a photo of the three of us together. I bought a round of Gaelic coffee, and Dave a second round. It was a great and spontaneous way to celebrate.

# A Few Facts

The following facts may be of interest:

During my journey I camped 32 nights in the wild, spent 37 nights at camping sites, and stayed for 27 nights in B & Bs; I passed through 17 counties, 56 hamlets, 121 villages, 44 towns, five cities (Truro, Bath, Lichfield, Edinburgh and Perth), and crossed four major bridges. In further detail, I visited 10 museums, 7 Iron Age villages/forts, 33 churches (1 Catholic), 4 cathedrals (Truro, Bath, Lichfield, Dornoch), 3 abbeys, 5 castles; and saw 25 memorials, 14 monuments, 4 holy wells, 6 fountains, 4 waterfalls, 2 follies, and 3 stocks. I also visited a vineyard, two cheese makers, a sweet factory, Pitlochry Highland Games, Peebles Arts Festival, Hadrian's Wall, Abbotsford stately home, and Blair Athol, Tomatin and Glenmorangie distilleries.

I enjoyed 42 pub and restaurant meals, either lunch or dinner, visited 35 tea-rooms eating 8 cream teas, and consumed 87 choc bars.

Amongst the wildlife I saw were snakes, snails and slugs, swallows, heron, deer, fox, buzzards, pheasant, mice, butterflies, flying ants, midges, plagues of black flies, grouse, kestrel, vole, spiders, bees, caterpillars, a toad, swans, weasel, stout, hedgehog, grouse, black rabbits, geese, ducks, frogs, dragonflies, hawks, skua, a mole, seals, seagulls, wasps.

Drinking a pint of real ale after a hard day's walk became such a pleasurable pursuit that I became a bit of a connoisseur on the subject and was always looking for new beers to taste. Altogether I visited a total of 105 pubs and consumed 285 pints of beer of 83 different varieties. Although difficult to pick out the best from such a large batch of great brews I sampled, I have particularly fond memories of the following: Cotleigh Tawny Bitter, Wadworth 6X, Flowers Original, Greene King Abbot Ale and also their King's Champion, Riverhead Redbrook Premium, Vaux's Waggle Dance, Castle Eden Ale, Timothy Taylor Landlord, Theakston Old Peculier, Border Farne Island, Caledonian 80, Orkney Dark Island, Moulin Old Remedial, and Tomintoul Wild Cat.

Of the many pubs I visited I would pick out the following for special mention: Sturt Arms pub, near Launceston - own Sturt ale and good food; Butterleigh Inn, Butterleigh - delightful, excellent beer, Egon Ronay food; Mount Inn pub, Stanton - ploughmans, very good; Bird in Hand, Henley-in-Arden - excellent beer and food; Greyhound, Colwich - good beer, nice place; Black Lion, Cheddleton - lunch, good pub; Knot Inn, Rushton - good pub; Riverhead Brewery Tap, Marsden - excellent beer, good place; Ward's Great Western pub, near Marsden - good lunch; White Lion Hotel, Hebden Bridge - good; Tan Hill Inn - cozy, middle of nowhere, good beer, highest pub at 1,732ft; Ancient Unicorn Inn, Bowes - dinner, good food and beer, friendly; George & Dragon, Garrigill - dinner, good; Moulin Inn, Pitlochry - excellent beer, food and service, busy; The Old Bridge Inn, Aviemore - good beer, food and service, entertainment; Blackfriars, Inverness - excellent beer; Eagle Hotel, Dornoch - good food, friendly.

My equipment consisted of the following (including what I wore!):

Eurohike Adventure 75 litre rucksack
Eurohike 220 tent
Survival bag
Sleeping bag and sleeping bag liner
Sleeping mat
2 water bottles
Clothing consisting of: sun hat, woollen cap, 2 pairs trousers, 1 pair
    overtrousers, 2 shirts, 1 sweater, Vander anorak, 2 pairs over
    socks, 3 pairs socks, 2 vests, 1 thermal vest, 2 pairs
    underpants, 3 handkerchiefs, 1 pair Berghaus boots, belt
Toilet bag containing: razor and 2 blades, mirror, tooth brush and
    paste, soap, comb and separate plastic bag containing foot
    treatment items—powder, pressure point pads, animal wool,
    anti-septic cream, blister pads
Towel
Nixwax polish
Freesole (boot repair)
Hand tissues
Cooking equipment consisting of: Coleman stove and gas cylinder,
    spare cylinder, two billycans, mug, Puritabs, knife, fork, spoon,
    Victorinex penknife, two lighters
Trowel
Provisions (Cuppa soup, Cappuccino, chocolate, dates, rice, mung
    dahl, vegetables, cheese, ginger)
Map case, Silva compass, motoring atlas pages, Ordnance Survey
    maps, central route pages from *Land's End to John O'Groats*
Writing pad, diary, note-book, biros
Camera and spare film
Torch
Whistle
Length of string
Safety pins
Water-proof watch